Resil

with
NeuroBiology Reprogramming™

Ultimate Resilience for Personal & Professional Success

Dr. Dugast

All rights reserved.

The contents of this book are trademarked, and no parts thereof may be reproduced in any form, stored in any retrieval system, or transmitted in any form by any means—electronic, mechanical, photocopy, recording, or otherwise—without prior written permission of the author.

Copyright © 2017 Dr. Dugast

PERMISSIONS

I am grateful to:

The use of 'What Are Your Values?', reproduced with permission from Mindtools at www.mindtools.com

The Story 'The Door' taken from *The Magic of Metaphor: 77 Stories for Teachers, Trainers & Thinkers* By Nick Owen © Nick Owen 2001 ISBN 9781899836703

Diagrams Dr. Dugast

Cover photo 123FR

Cover design Murray Mc Carthy

Editing Robert Kidd at EditFast

Author photo Aya Watada

ISBN-13: 978-1541130678
ISBN-10: 1541130677

DEDICATION

To Azaro

CONTENTS

Note to Reader ix
Foreword xi

PART ONE
Buddha-Style Awareness and Peace of Mind with Integrated Practical Awareness (I.P.A.)

CHAPTER 1
I.P.A. Level I: Basic Practice 1
Mindfulness Reloaded 2
Developing Integrated Practical Awareness 5
Tool One—The B.B.C. Practice 10
Multitasking: The Enemy of Presence 23
Exercise—Multitasking 24
Let's Talk Story!—Hawaiian Tradition 30
Practice Recap 31

CHAPTER 2
I.P.A. Level II: Intermediate Practice 33
Resilience—Freedom and Strength in Unity 34
Tool Two—The B.B.M.E. Practice 36
Anchoring Your State of Peace with a Physical Gesture 41
Know Thyself—So You Can Free Thyself 44
Building Resilience 47
The Wealth Factor 53
Let's Talk Story! 55
Practice Recap 1 56
Practice Recap 2 57

CHAPTER 3
I.P.A. Level III: Advanced Practice — 59
Reclaiming Your Power — 60
Exercise—Personal Inventory — 61
Let's Talk Story! — 66
Practice Recap — 67

CHAPTER 4
Time Resilience — 69
What Time Is It? — 70
Exercise—Part 1: Where Do You Live? — 76
Exercise—Part 2: Mastering Time and Preparing for Mental Resilience — 78
Q&A — 81
Let's Talk Story! — 86
Practice Recap — 87
Part One Full I.P.A. Practice Recap — 89

PART TWO
NeuroBiology Reprogramming™

CHAPTER 5
N.B.R. Level One: Mental Resilience — 95
The Nature and Purpose of the Mind — 99
The Anatomy of the Mind — 104
A Diagram of You — 111
The Practice: NeuroBiology Reprogramming™—Level One — 113
Preparation for the Process — 115
The Pranayama Breath — 119
When and Why to Use NeuroBiology Programming™ — 126
Q&A — 141
Let's Talk Story! — 155
Practice Recap — 156

CHAPTER 6
Taking NeuroBiology Reprogramming™ on the Road — 157
Exercise—Part 1: How Smooth Is Your Ride? — 158
Exercise—Part 2: Identify the Programs/Beliefs — 164
Let's Talk Story! — 168
Practice Recap — 169

CHAPTER 7
N.B.R. Level Two: Emotional Resilience — 171
The Nature of Emotions — 176
Attributes of the Emotional Body — 177
The Science Behind Emotional Resilience — 186
How to Make Use of the Emotional Body — 193
Applying NeuroBiology Reprogramming™ to the Emotional Body — 196
Exercise—Where Do You Live Emotionally? — 198
Q&A — 223
Let's Talk Story! — 235
Practice Recap — 236

CHAPTER 8
N.B.R. Level Three: Physical Resilience — 237
What Is the Physical Body? — 238
You — 239
My Experience with Cancer — 241
Nature of the Physical Body — 244
The Nature of Worldly Success — 246
Q&A — 250
Resilience and Self-Esteem Tools — 261
Practice Recap — 265

Full N.B.R. Practice Recap Part 1 — 266
Full N.B.R. Practice Recap Part 2 — 267

PART THREE
The Master Plan

CHAPTER 9
The Heart of Leadership	273
Building Resilience in Leadership	278
Essential Leadership Skill n.1: Communication	279
Q&A	284
4 Ways to Prepare for Clear Communication	290
Essential Leadership Skill n.2: Personal Values and Standards	293
Exercise—Your Personal Values	295
Resilience in Parenting	301
Let's Talk Story!	305
Chapter Recap	306

CHAPTER 10
Reverse Engineering	307
Exercise—The Art of Asking Self-Empowering Questions	310
Master Tool	312
Parting Note	316
About the Author	319

Dear reader,

Did you ever play a game without knowing the rules? Probably not, as it wouldn't allow you to win it, and therefore not be so enjoyable.

In order to get all the resilience you need, mental, emotional and physical, in daily life as well as in business, you need to know a few simple things, in particular how your mind works. This is because it is at the origin of your whole experience. Getting a handle on it is a lot simpler than you might imagine or might have been told, and acquiring the knowledge you need, along with a simple few tools, will make all the difference and restore or instil all the resilience you could ever wish for.

Whether you need resilience to create a thriving business, get your dream job, keep or cultivate a leadership position, you will find this book helpful and relevant.

You will find it equally useful if you are out of work and need to get back on track, or have been experiencing repeated challenges that you haven't been able to get beyond. You may be experiencing a familiar plateau that is proving hard to tackle, or perhaps you want to take things to the next level and are concerned that you may not have all the pieces you need to do so.

Or perhaps, you already have the success you sought out, but have now realized that it does not fulfil you in the way you expected that it would. This book is designed for you; as success, no matter what it means to you, is always an inside job first.

Although there is a professional slant on this book, you will be able to apply it for your personal life. This is because we are focusing on you, and you are at the centre of your own life. It includes examples and case studies based on personal and professional concerns from some of my clients and students; although, all names have been changed to preserve confidentiality.

I have even included some information to develop resilience in parenting, because the truth is that all areas of your life interconnect. Once you have a way to gain all the resilience you need, which is to say developing self-mastery, you will want to adapt it to all areas of your life so you can deepen your sense of fulfilment in all things.

The method is precise, and the tools are few.

One more thing, if doubting yourself is something you do, from today onward... drop it! You are absolutely 'on cue' holding the very thing that can help you in your hands right now. May this be a confirmation of your ability to get exactly what you need when you need it. The truth, as you will find out while we journey together, is that you are powerful and amazing, and that success, no matter which kind you seek, is much closer than you think. These are not compliments but facts.

I wrote this book for you, and sincerely hope that you will enjoy it and make good use of it.

Thank you for investing in yourself, and for taking some time aside to make it work for you.

You are far more powerful than you were led to believe

FOREWORD

This book contains what I teach during seminars and online classes. Personal science is a very large subject, and there are many methods to choose from, which can be incredibly confusing. The last 30 years have allowed me to research, practise, refine, and transmit these 3 steps, a method I call NeuroBiology Reprogramming™, which is what I am sharing with you in this book, and how you are going to get ultimate resilience.

The book is organised in two parts. The first is designed to help you develop increased awareness and permanent peace of mind. You will also be able to reclaim the parts of you that you left along the way, due to past events and situations that may still be draining your resilience and personal power today.

The second part is concerned with literally upgrading your own mental software. First, I will show you how to easily clear any limiting beliefs, and then harness your mind to regain control of it and use it as the amazing creative tool that it is. With this, you will be able to access your untapped potential, and have access to unlimited inspiration and all the benefits that it can produce, when applied to the areas you would like to develop, improve, transform, or take to the next level.

The two parts combined emulate the advice carved in stone eons ago: "Know Thyself". This advice is pertinent to understanding the rules of the game and gaining access to a key for playing and winning the game of life and, with it, the game of business.

I find that the 80/20 Pareto principle works very well here to illustrate that personal or professional success in any given area of your choosing is built upon

20% skill and 80% *internal wiring*. This *internal wiring* is made from the mental-emotional predisposition we all have, and is the foundation upon which rock-solid resilience can be developed.

Although you will actually not be the same person by the time you finish reading this book, as reading about your personal power is, of course, fascinating, I highly recommend you practise what is in it, so you can derive maximum benefit.

> *"Knowledge without practice is useless.*
> *Practice without knowledge is dangerous."*
> — Confucius

This is what will insure that you benefit from the fastest and most steady results. It is designed and adapted to the busiest of lives, and the practices shared will yield instant results, the minute you use them. By the end of this book, you will 'Know Thyself' and have a practice that will take no more than 3-6 minutes each day.

*NeuroBiology Reprogramming™ is also available as a practitioner and teacher online and in-person training.

PART ONE

BUDDHA-STYLE AWARENESS
AND
PEACE OF MIND
WITH
INTEGRATED PRACTICAL AWARENESS
(I.P.A.)

I.P.A. LEVEL I—BASIC PRACTICE
I.P.A. LEVEL II—INTERMEDIATE PRACTICE
I.P.A. LEVEL III—ADVANCED PRACTICE

CHAPTER 1

INTEGRATED PRACTICAL AWARENESS

I.P.A. LEVEL I: BASIC PRACTICE

"Knowing others is intelligence; knowing yourself is true wisdom. Mastering others is strength. Mastering yourself is true power."
— Lao Tzu

MINDFULNESS RELOADED

How to Make Use of an Ancient Practice in a Hyper-Modern World

The foundation to being able to access maximum resilience is rooted in solid, daily self-discipline. It begins by being able to be as consciously aware or as 'present' as can be, as often as possible. The benefit of this commitment is threefold.

First, it allows us to have access to peace of mind at will, which makes it easier to sail through daily stresses and challenges.

Second, it affords us the necessary inner calm and self-confidence that comes from knowing how to access our inner most resourcefulness instantly. Aside from the benefit of not drowning in overwhelm or overload, it means that we can remain efficient, recognise and seize solutions and opportunities as they appear.

Third, as we develop a sense of self-mastery, our life quality improves, which means that we feel energised. Having more 'mojo' is key to having what it takes to pursue the necessary steps to close the gap between where we are in the moment and what we want to achieve or experience. All of this contributes to developing resilience.

To develop daily peace of mind, there are two main practices which can help us in powerful ways.

One is to meditate daily.

The other is to practise a form of 'walking meditation', which is also known as mindful living. This is precisely what you will be able to do with the method that I have developed, called Integrated Practical Awareness (I.P.A.). For some people, the practice of meditating is simply not an option, as they do not feel they have the time nor the patience to sit still for extended periods of time. When I became a busy entrepreneur, I must admit that I turned into such a person, although, I had been a practitioner for many years. I am glad it happened the way that it did, because it allowed me to adapt an ancient practice to a process that can be used with equal and perhaps even superior benefits, no matter how busy or impatient you may be.

I.P.A. is a set of two steps, designed to get you back to a state of calm and resourcefulness instantly, no matter how challenging the moment may be. This will help you to restore or develop your own confidence and self-esteem. These practices could accurately be described as your 'safety rope' as they will allow you to pull yourself out of the most challenging of situations, without losing your ability to respond in the best possible way. Life will keep on happening, so the trick is to be able to handle it with grace and gusto, and turn whatever happens into something you can use to keep building your resilience level. On the pleasurable side, these simple practices will deepen your sense of gratitude and contribute to improving your life quality.

The two steps included in I.P.A. also offer the necessary preparation to make use of a third step so you can develop bulletproof resilience. With these, you will have access to solid inner guidance and be able to make use of a superior mind, or 'inspired thinking', at will.

If You Are Going to Choose One . . . I.P.A. Is the One!

If you have limited time each day, I recommend you choose I.P.A. over regular sitting-down meditation. This is because you spend many hours 'in action', more than you could in sitting-down meditating. Or, at least, if one is a member of society and not a hermit living in a cave on a mountaintop!

If you decide to keep practising meditation and use I.P.A., you will, without a doubt, derive maximum benefit. What I find with some of my clients and students is that, once they use this form of 'meditation in action', they naturally see the value in taking some time out to do some sitting-down meditation. Sometimes, it happens as a natural occurrence.

Another nuance that is not so familiar regarding sitting-down meditation is that it is a male-based practice. While I cannot expand on this subject in this book, I can give you a brief outline, which is that, while we all have access to masculine and feminine energies, and whether you are a man or a woman, if your overriding essence is feminine, your meditation may take the form of movement rather than that of stillness.[1] So dancing or singing, for example, could be your form of meditation.

DEVELOPING INTEGRATED PRACTICAL AWARENESS

Integrated Practical Awareness is the ability to gain, develop and practise internal and external awareness.

Why Gain Internal Awareness?

Aside from having access to peace of mind at will, which is a feat in itself, using I.P.A. will prepare you for the rest of the processes given in this book. It will be useful for shedding some light on what limits you have been imposing upon yourself. For example, if you have experienced repeated challenges in a particular area of your life, it will provide the *insight* necessary to recognise how your own values and beliefs contribute to your direct environment, and what beliefs may be in the way of what you want, so you can clear them. We will do this in the second part of this book.

Finally, increased internal awareness will restore your ability to be somewhat in control of your own mind. This will empower you, as everything you create in your life begins in your mind.

---

[1] See '1:1 Extraordinary Unions' at www.drdugast.com

Why Gain External Awareness?

Increased internal awareness naturally allows us to have clearer external awareness. This allows us to be more receptive, productive and relevant as there is less involvement or focus on personal concerns. This can help us to identify and resolve challenges in a more dispassionate way, which can be crucial in business decisions. Greater external awareness can also allow us to recognise opportunities in the moment, or even ahead of time, or, for example, to help us 'retool' in the right timing to make sure that your own business or department, if you are a leader, is fully resilient.

Using I.P.A. in the Organisation

If you work in an organisation, you may have noticed that incentives such as employee engagement programs or bonus schemes do not have the power to truly transform the work culture. This is because real personal motivation and the desire to contribute has to be a personal decision. While most of us were raised to believe that our external situation or circumstances are the cause of our internal feelings—and our success or our failure—we now have all the research and the evidence we need to understand that this is not so.

Success, or any positive change we want to experience, is created from the inside out. You will find that, as you take care of yourself and develop your own practice, you will have far more of an impact than trying to convince people of something they may not be able to hear. In reality, external challenges and hardships, especially if recurrent, are the cues and signals that internal adjustments are required. Different results can and will be experienced, both within yourself and within your department or your business, as you commit to your own personal self-mastery.

Become a Leader

Whether you actually work in a leadership capacity or not, I invite you to take or reclaim a leading role in your own life. Why would I suggest this? Simply because no one else can live the life that was given to you. So you might as well step into your given role, rather than keep playing as an 'extra' in your own movie, your own life. If you have been waiting for someone to save you, grab a mirror and look into it: you're it!

If you do work in a leadership capacity, a good exercise would be for you to ask yourself how you define leadership. Self-inquiry is a powerful way to evaluate if what you believe, meaning your own values, beliefs and standards, really serve your purpose. Some of these values may need to be shifted, and new ones may need to be installed or developed. While there are many different styles of leadership, the kind that this book is aiming at is inspirational in nature. This is the kind of leadership most in demand right now, in a world that is evolving and including consciousness. I call this the 'Heart of Leadership', which is the ability to inspire people to deliver their best, as naturally happens when they feel a sense of growth and contribution in their respective duties.

Motivational leadership is good, and definitely a step above dictatorial leadership, but it has a short lifespan, due to its intended influence, which is aimed at affecting us from the 'outside in'. Change has to come from within, at least if it is to be fundamental, and have the momentum necessary to create the kind of steady progress that leads to success. Hence this book being aimed at the individual, even if your intention is to affect the whole. There is a whole section dedicated to leadership skills toward the end of this book, but for now, let's focus on developing internal and external awareness with I.P.A.

Adapting I.P.A. to Handle Daily Stresses

Before we can deal effectively with stress, we must first identify the nature of it. The causes of stress will be many, but its nature is only one. Being busy is often mistaken for being stressed. Yet, one doesn't necessarily go with the other. You could be really busy and be quite tired, but not stressed in the least. In fact, you could be at the beginning of an enterprise you have just created, using your talent, and doing something you love, working an 80-100-hour week. This is far from abnormal at the beginning of a venture. Or, you could have very little going on and feel completely stressed and overwhelmed.

While different stresses affect different individuals, depending on their personal level of resilience, the mechanism is the same: stress is created the moment we attempt to control an external situation that we cannot change, or that has already come to pass.

As we move through this book, you will realise that stress, like any other emotional internal state, is a result and not a cause. It is the result of a thought or a belief. Therefore, refusing to accept what has already come to pass can only disempower us. Trying to resolve it solely using external means is futile. Stress begins with a simple phrase such as 'This can't be happening . . .' or 'I can't cope with this . . .' or 'This is killing me!'

While we certainly have limited control on some external situations, sometimes none at all, we can certainly choose our reactions, and what meaning we attach to them. These give us the powerful mental images with which we create our life, and the next set of events.

Being able to get a handle on this is essential, which is why you will find I.P.A. invaluable. Having instant access to your own internal resources spells the difference between feeling that you cannot cope—and going into overwhelm—or winning the day, no matter what.

TOOL ONE—THE B.B.C. PRACTICE

This first practice is a very simple process that will afford you all the benefits of meditation. With daily practise, you will gain distance and respite from the tyrannical mind-emotion duo. I call it 'tuning in to your B.B.C.', which is your Body Breath Connection. It is a very simple method, allowing you to transform your personal triggers into allies and reminders. This practice will insure that you can turn any perceived adversity to your own advantage. Guaranteed.

Practising the B.B.C. is particularly useful when:

- You are in a crisis or in a critical situation.
- You have just heard some difficult or bad news.
- You are extremely busy and only have a few seconds to pull yourself together.
- You feel the need for an immediate boost of vital life force or energy.
- You simply need a break. There is only one of you around, after all!
- You need to reduce your stress levels in the moment (job interview, meeting, making an important decision, meeting a date, etc.).
- You need to access your higher mind to come up with an answer or an innovative solution quickly.

How to Tune in to Your B.B.C.—Part One

1. Put your attention on your breathing. Don't alter it in any way, simply pay attention to it. As you witness it, you may find yourself naturally inhaling and exhaling a little deeper, which is highly beneficial.

2. Put your attention on your feet. Feel your shoes on your feet and feel the ground beneath them. This allows you to become 'grounded' or 'earthed'.

It doesn't matter what floor your office or flat is on, there are foundations to the building. You are connected.

Benefit of this practice: as you shift your focus from being engaged in ideas that may be stressing you to tuning in to your B.B.C., your mind-emotion is getting a little respite.

Do not be deceived by the simplicity of this practice. It yields many benefits, even if you only do it for a few seconds. The success lies in repeated practise.

Take this moment to practise this simple step now.

Next, let's make sure you use this simple practice as often as possible.

Creating Tailor-Made Reminders—Part Two

Tuning in to your B.B.C. is very simple. However, it is not easy, because, until the mind is trained, it will not remember to practise it. To insure that you can remember to practise your B.B.C., we are going to set up some "anchors" in the form of a quick list of things that usually have the power to irritate you. Each thing you put on that list will then become your cue, your reminder to practise. This is precisely how you will also be able to turn any kind of adversity to your own advantage, and develop Buddha-style awareness and peace of mind.

For now, please identify the petty, daily annoyances that contribute to your losing contact with your source of calm, intellectual power, resourcefulness, and well-being. Please don't look for world issues. You need to find repetitive, small and petty daily irritants, things that usually provoke you to lose your cool and react. Write down 5-10 irritants or more. In this case, the more the merrier!

These can literally be anything, such as waiting for the light to go green in traffic, waiting for your computer to load or update, finding dirty cups at the coffee station, being caught in queues in shops, delays in a flight or train schedule, a co-worker doing something repetitive that irritates you, etc.! You get the idea.

I get particularly annoyed when:
-
-
-
-
-

When your list is made, use anything that is on it as a reminder to practise your B.B.C. It is as simple as that. We are doing this because, if you are like most of us, we encounter a wide array of irritating factors in the course of a day. If every time any of these petty annoyances happen, you choose to use it as a reminder to practise your B.B.C., you will win the day! In short, you are in line for serious self-mastery. You will begin to live from a place of constant resourcefulness rather than reactedness. This means that you will be able to access peace of mind, at will, no matter what, using the most unlikely of reminders. This will help you to avoid conflict, and may even contribute to resolving it if it has already started.

Do not dismiss this step on account of it being so simple. Life is simple, solutions are always there; it is the mind that has learned to make things unnecessarily complicated.

What if the Nature of Your Experience Is More Joyous than Irritating?

This is a recurrent question I get during seminars, and a great one, because you can do the same with things that delight you. Having more occasions for joy or happiness is a wonderful thing, of course. Strangely enough, having these wonderful feelings can become as much of a challenge as the daily irritants, especially if we cling to them. This is partly because, when feelings or situations are really good, we want to hang on to them for fear of losing them. Yet, the effect of holding on tight to anything is that it can become stifled. This can stop it from developing or being taken to the next level. This can be difficult to grasp, because we are 'programmed' to believe that only the positive emotions are useful. The truth is that the nature of our experience is made from ever-changing probabilities and possibilities, and it is not so much about good or bad but rather of being able to use the experience to develop our potential and, with it, our resilience level. Go ahead and write some things that delight you below.

I absolutely love when:

-
-
-
-
-

The Illusion of 'Balance'

There is nothing static in life. Whatever you can think of, your marriage, your business or your own human potential, it is either growing or spiralling down. Seeking complete balance, or the end of all challenges, is futile, unless you are looking to exhale your last breath. Let us agree here that this is not something to strive for just now!

The nature of reality is impermanence itself. I can't think of an occasion where you might not make use of your own internal resources to grow and learn something. So if you are willing to use times of boundless joy as well as rough times to practise, you will find that you can liberate yourself from most concepts, including that of 'balance'.

Life happens for you and not to you. Being able to experience this will naturally deepen the quality of your life. As you tune in to your B.B.C., you will find that you can be more present to yourself and in your relationships, which will give you self-confidence, as you will get a far better response from the people with whom you interact. The more you develop a sense of trust in yourself, the more you will attract occasions that will consolidate this new truth. Your potential will keep on unfolding.

The 'trick' is to become as aware as you can, as often as possible. This is why your list of anchors can be as long as you want, with things that annoy or delight you. This is a win-win situation, that everyone benefits from, beginning with you.

Success Is Near

I personally guarantee you that if you practise your B.B.C. at every occasion for as little as for the next few hours, you will feel enough benefit that you will want to keep practising. Everything is cumulative, including peace of mind! Each time you tune in to your B.B.C., you are strengthening a new neural pathway in your mind. Soon enough, this will be a new learned habit, and like any habit, it will be so easy to practise, you won't even have to think of it consciously.

This is a quantum leap in getting ready to be able to control your own mind. A game-changer.

Opportunities in Hiding

Although we would all rather do without, crises and challenges naturally arise to give us a chance to rise above them. They often represent a defining moment when we get the opportunity to choose between evolving into more of who we really are, which is pure potential, or feeling defeated. Resolving a situation or achieving a goal is almost never the most important in itself, although, of course, both of these can come with a tremendous sense of relief and completion. The all-important factor is the person we become through the process.

There will always be challenges to overcome. In fact, these often cause us to dig deeper into our potential and resourcefulness, which is why I prefer to rename crises and challenges *evolutionary drivers*. Don't worry, by the time you have learnt the full version of NeuroBiology Reprogramming™, you will be able to be resilient in any circumstances. Right now, we are starting where it makes the most sense: at the beginning.

The Physiological Response to the B.B.C.

As you pay attention to feeling your feet on the ground, and as you focus on your breathing, you are giving your nervous system an immediate break. Rather than fuelling a fight-or-flight response, which produces an abundance of stress hormones—epinephrine and cortisol—your mind gets a moment's respite, during which the 'happy neurotransmitters'—serotonin, dopamine, oxytocin—are released into your body. This mind-emotion process is at the base of our health and well-being.

Each time that you practise your B.B.C., you are training your neurobiology to respond differently to stress. This is very important because stress, the fight-or-flight response, is only meant to last up to 90 seconds. It is designed to literally reroute the blood and energy from your centre—your gut—to fuel your arms and legs, in preparation to bolt away from danger. The body is not built to sustain a repeated or an ongoing fight-or-flight state. A daily state of stress is the root cause of many illnesses. There is much neuroscientific research available today that illustrates what I am describing here.[2] We understand how our own internal wiring—our mind-emotions connection—greatly affects our state of health and energy. We know that repeated stress is at the root of so many illnesses. Yet, we can

---

[2] *The Biology of Belief* by Dr. Bruce Lipton / *Molecules of Emotion* by Dr. Candace Pert.

prevent results that are nothing less than catastrophic without using allopathic medicine, by simply developing enough self-discipline to practise the B.B.C.

The other important—although, more subtle—side effect of repeated stress is that, when we are in fight-or-flight, our gut is depleted of the blood supply it usually sustains, which means that we are disabling ourselves from one of our most important attributes: our gut feeling. This is a very useful attribute that can be applied to many areas of our life, including our business affairs. This 'internal compass' is literally an asset that no leader or entrepreneur can afford to disregard.

So even if tuning in to your B.B.C. only lasts a few seconds each time you remember to practise it, it is long enough for your neurobiology to get a little respite, and to learn a different way of operating. As you momentarily reconnect to your inner source through the B.B.C. practice, you are allowing in the single most important nutrient for your body-mind: your breath.

Why Is the Breath so Important?

You may think that the most important nutrient is food or even water, but while you can go without food or water for a number of days, you can only go without breath for a short few minutes. This makes breath our most precious resource. This is also why it is the focus of most healing techniques, therapies, self-discipline and spiritual practices. Yet, it is one that is nearly always overlooked, and the first to be affected when stress arises. The breath can shorten and even stop for a few seconds when we are worried or afraid, trying not to make mistakes, when hearing bad news, or simply when we are so focused on our computer screen that we breathe very shallow breaths.

When breath becomes shallow, it means that oxygen supply is very short, which can contribute to the cause of an array of physical problems, including headaches and back pain. This is particularly prominent for people whose work involves computers. While the body is amazing, thankfully run by intelligence that is far beyond our intellect, a force that I call Natural Intelligence, it is none the less in deficit when not given what it needs on a daily basis. Sustained lack of adequate breathing, or oxygen, is enough to hinder clear thinking or vibrant health, or the ability to unpack our innate potential and create the success we have in mind.

However, tuning in to your B.B.C. and putting your attention on your breath will reconnect you as a whole, and relax your whole nervous system. Breathing literally carries supplies, energy and information to your cells. With daily practise, the B.B.C. can literally help you to unlock the inherent regenerative power and expanded potential that is already within you. This is particularly useful if your work or choice of career demands that you access an inspired and innovative mindset.

7 Good Reasons to Tune in to Your B.B.C.

Practising your B.B.C. for a few seconds several times a day instantly contributes to:

1. Relaxing your muscles overall.

2. Lowering your blood pressure.

3. Slowing down your heart rate.

4. Reducing your stress levels instantly.

5. Slowing down your own breathing rhythm, which will allow you to relax deeper.

6. Your body healing itself as it is momentarily 'unplugged' from the mind-emotion's tyrannical influence.

7. Your ability to access your own natural resources, responses, ideas, and solutions.

As already mentioned, the breath is the central pillar of mindfulness and self-discipline. It is the centrepiece of many spiritual traditions because it is literally the conduit of life itself. This life force is also known as 'mana', 'chi' or 'prana' depending on different traditions. It is the imperceptible link, the fragile bridge between life and death, and the fuel that allows you to partake in the amazing gifts that were given to you: your life and the potential to unpack it.

The breath is also the vehicle through which the

mind, the emotions and the body connect to the awesome power that created us, Natural Intelligence. Whatever anyone believes, whether there is a preference for the religious, spiritual or scientific medium, the fact is that there is a power that is larger than us, from our origin and at our disposal. The good thing is that being able to use it doesn't rely on anything else but a personal decision. It is available right within you, on tap, 24/7, and it provides you with the surest and most everlasting source of well-being, peace, joy, inspiration, and resilience.

Every time you tune in to your B.B.C., you are effectively accessing and reconnecting with your inherent Natural Intelligence. Like anything you do repeatedly, this too is cumulative. Before long, connecting to this Natural Intelligence can become a habit, and therefore give you the potential and the information you need to thrive. If you ever sought an ally, a beloved, a constant source of wisdom, or an excellent business partner, you certainly have one when you connect to this awesome source of Natural Intelligence. This is what I mean by your superior mind or your higher intelligence. The conscious mind is great, particularly when it is connected to its origin and creator, Natural Intelligence.

Tuning in to Your Own B.B.C. While You Interact with Others

While this may sound counterproductive at first, tuning in to your B.B.C. is highly beneficial while you interact with others. Having more internal awareness means that you will not only notice what is going on in you, but also around you. This can make you more receptive and more empathic to your interlocutor. We often hear people talk but we are often not really listening. This is because being self-absorbed with our own problems, or with what we are going to say next, makes it difficult to be present. You can be certain that your interlocutor can feel it, even if they cannot put words on it. Often, they can. No one likes to talk with someone who is absent, or mentally 'elsewhere'. It results in them feeling unheard: they are!

Tuning in to your B.B.C. while you are interacting with someone will insure that they feel heard. Furthermore, and particularly if you want to find a solution to a problem, you will find that being truly present during a conversation means that the person in front of you can often come up with their own solution. This is because when presence is part of mutual communication, it brings in a dimension of self-reflection for the person who is doing the talking. It is a little bit like thinking aloud in the presence of an ally. At the very least, they will feel valued and validated, which is a boost in itself, and a very valuable skill to develop for any leader. We will explore more leadership-style communication toward the end of the book.

MULTITASKING: THE ENEMY OF PRESENCE

Multitasking, also known as switch-tasking, is very tempting, especially when you are so busy. You might even say you want to keep on doing it, yet you despise it when you are at the receiving end of it. We have all come into contact with people who choose to text while we interact with them, whether it is with colleagues at work, friends while we are out, or with our own kids at home. It is unpleasant in any and all cases.

Another form of switch-tasking is doing several things at once, such as writing an email while answering a call. The illusion is that we are achieving more in the same amount of time, but it turns out not to be so.

Research conducted in Stanford University and Sussex University both came to the same conclusion: multitasking is counterproductive. It was studied and proven to literally reduce the grey matter in the brain, which means that it takes us longer to achieve what we set out to do. To add to this, it turns out that we also make more mistakes when we multitask. As if these weren't enough negative consequences, research shows that switch-tasking encourages attention deficit and even reduces our I.Q. (intellectual quotient) by up to 15 points, thereby reducing our thinking capacity and attention span to that of an 8-9-year-old child! Better to see it for yourself, of course, so I invite you to take a few moments to do the following exercise and see your scores. And remember, winning this one means . . . you lose!

EXERCISE
Multitasking

This exercise is inspired from the work of Dave Crenshaw, author of *The Myth of Multitasking*.

You need: A piece of paper and a stopwatch. Draw a box similar to the one below. The exercise is done in two parts.

First part: Have your stopwatch ready, and start timing yourself as you write the following two lines, one at time: 'I am excellent at multitasking', followed by numbers 1 to 26 right below it. See the example below. Keep a note of your timing.

I am excellent at multitasking

1 2 3 4 5 6 7 8 9 10 11 12 13 14 15 16 17 18 19 20 21 22 23 24 25 26

Your turn:

Second part: You will be doing the same exercise, only this time, you write one letter at a time, and one number at a time, one below the other. Once again, time yourself from beginning to end of the exercise.

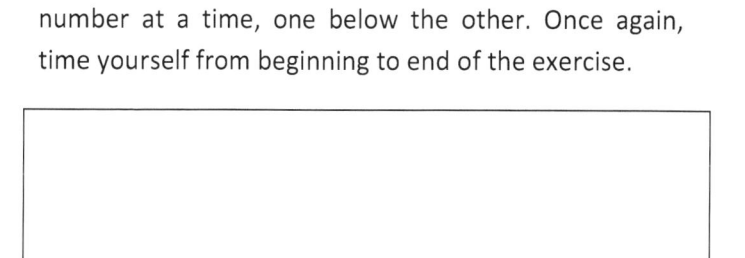

How did you score? Between you and me, when I did this for the first time, it took me 28 seconds for the first part, and 48 seconds for the second part! I even made a spelling mistake to go with it. Most people take longer doing the second part, sometimes double the time. This proves that multitasking is not as effective as we thought it was, and having raised three kids while being an entrepreneur, I would have sworn that this was the only way to get things done!

If you kept the same time, it means that you are really in trouble, because while you may have become a 'productivity machine' it is probably taking its toll somewhere else in your personal life. Now might be a good time to reflect and see where you can be more present in your life.

The Real Damage of Multitasking

As if all of this was not damaging enough, multitasking also means that it reduces our ability to be present to ourselves and others. While this could be considered a hindrance at work, but be easily corrected by simply choosing to do one thing at a time, it can cost us far more in our personal life. A common symptom of this is the level of presence we bring to our personal relationships, with our beloved and/or our children. We may be physically present but completely elsewhere in our mind.

Although it may be tempting to brush this aside as something that is trivial, not important or non-damaging, I propose the contrary. Personal relationships, beginning with the one we have with ourselves, are the root of our whole experience, and very much influence the quality of our life. Any part of our experience affects all others. It is very difficult to carry out 'business as usual' when we are deeply dissatisfied in our relationship with our spouse, for example. There really is no separation; we are a whole being, and one thing affects another. This is the nature of reality. When we feel internally fragmented, in our mind-emotion and our body, we are effectively 'disconnected'. This means that we are not as good company as we could be with the people that matter most to us, nor as efficient in our professional life. This often translates as a feeling of being in the right place at the wrong time, or even worse, in the wrong place and at the wrong time.

This contributes to widening the already existing internal split in the mind, that we will resolve in the second part of this book. This can leave us feeling dissatisfied, frustrated and lacking self-esteem.

Statements like 'What is it all about?' or 'What's the point?' or 'What is the purpose to it all?' or 'Will this ever stop?' are prevalent at such times. This is when our resilience reaches an all-time low.

Common Fragmentation Scenarios Include:

- o Having dinner with the family while mentally replaying a work-related event, imagining what you will say next time.

- o Trying to spend quality time with your children, but being mentally elsewhere.

- o Being at the office, feeling guilty for not paying enough attention to your spouse or children.

- o Sitting in the office, wishing to be elsewhere.

- o In bed with your spouse and thinking about someone else.

- o Being outdoors playing sports, worried about some financial transactions or investments.

- o Being among friends, feeling lonely, wishing you were back home.

- o Being in a relationship, feeling alone, wishing or waiting for someone else, or better, to appear.

3 Powerful Antidotes to Multitasking and Fragmentation

Whenever you feel 'fragmented', here is how you can take care of your internal wiring to feel calmer and more resilient, and connected to your source of power:

1. **Tune in to our own B.B.C.** as often as possible. It will contribute to bringing yourself back to the moment, body and mind together, which will make you feel better instantly. You will regain a sense of personal power, confidence, well-being and the people around you will certainly feel it, and your professional endeavours will prosper.

2. **Make it easy for yourself:** Choose to do one thing at a time!

3. **Just know** that one or two hours of your absolute presence with your spouse and/or children is worth a whole weekend 'trying' to engage with them while feeling fragmented, too busy to be there fully, or absent-minded.

How to Bring Up Mindful Children

A recurrent question I get during seminars is, as parents, how do we bring up mindful children? My answer is always that children are just fine. They are far wiser than us, as they enjoy a closer connection to Natural Intelligence than we do, or at least until we develop our own self-discipline.

The best course of action is to take care of ourselves, the same way that is recommended we do during the security announcement before any flight. "Put your oxygen mask to yourself first, then help your children."

As you may have noticed if you have some, children don't do what we say but, instead, duplicate what we do. Just as we did with our own parents, they learn to duplicate from our behaviour rather than words. We have all learnt most of the habits we have today, including our values and beliefs, while we were small children. All this information got recorded below conscious level, straight into our subconscious mind. This is why we act like our parents, and have similar qualities, limitations and results. We will study this extensively in the second part of this book, along with acquiring ways to delete even the deepest and oldest of mental/emotional family lineage.

For now, the point is to practise on yourself what you might be tempted to teach. I brought this example early on to describe how powerful your own decision to take care of yourself could be with your children, and your family at large. Taking care of yourself is primordial. It is a very worthwhile investment and not at all a selfish act. I would even go as far as to say that it is essential. This is precisely how you can set yourself and your children free from replicating unwanted patterns, no matter what they are.

LET'S TALK STORY!—HAWAIIAN TRADITION

'Talking story' is a Hawaiian tradition that some Elders still practise today, after food was shared together. I have the good fortune to have been adopted by such an Elder, and therefore share some of her custom.

At the end of each chapter, you will enjoy a flavour of this tradition as I will use multi-denominational spiritual traditions and the power of storytelling. I hope you enjoy it.

Inspired from Ancient Zen Teachings

Two Zen disciples sit together. One disciple is bragging about his own Master's extraordinary abilities to another disciple, who follows another Master.

'My Master can levitate, and at the same time write in the air with a brush, and have the characters appear on a piece of paper hundreds of feet away!'

'My Master too, is capable of extraordinary feats.'

'Really, what can YOUR Master DO?'

'When my Master sleeps, he sleeps. When he eats, he eats.'

CHAPTER 1—PRACTICE RECAP

Integrated Practical Awareness
I.P.A.—BASIC PRACTICE

Tuning in to your B.B.C.

1. Simply put your attention on your feet, and feel the ground beneath them. This allows you to become 'grounded' or 'earthed'. It doesn't matter what floor your office or flat is on, there are foundations to the building so this will work.

2. Note your own breathing. Don't alter it in any way, simply pay attention to it. As you observe it, you may find yourself inhaling and exhaling a little deeper, which is highly beneficial.

To make this simple practice highly useable through your busy day, use your list of anchors.

CHAPTER 2

INTEGRATED PRACTICAL AWARENESS

I.P.A. LEVEL II: INTERMEDIATE PRACTICE

"What a liberation to realize that the 'voice in my head' is not who I am. 'Who am I, then?' The one who sees that."
— Eckhart Tolle

RESILIENCE
FREEDOM AND STRENGTH IN UNITY

Over years of practise and working with people from many different cultures and backgrounds, I have seen that our lack of resilience has many faces, but only one root. As we have 'evolved' as a species, contributed to shaping the world around us, we have separated ourselves from the unity of our four attributes—physical, mental, emotional, and spiritual. This has taken a serious toll on our natural wisdom, and reduced our innate capacity to cope and, beyond this, to thrive to the fullest of our potential.

I propose that we put simplicity back into the equation, by remembering who we are, so we may be able to get a handle on what we can affect: ourselves. It was written that "a house divided cannot stand". This is a powerful analogy that lends itself well to reflect the connectedness, or lack thereof, of our own internal mechanism and, therefore, potential.

Many a great leaders throughout history have known and applied this concept to consolidate their winning strategy, and to make victory a more probable reality. Whether the intention is to keep a family together, an army united, a productive team in the work culture, or oneself 'whole', the greatest resilience anyone can ever avail of is rooted in one's own internal unity, first and foremost. Separation and fragmentation equal division. A division of our own power and potential. This may be experienced as a feeling of 'not being enough', or a feeling of 'entrapment' in a relationship or a job, or 'wanting out' of a present situation. Once unfulfillment sets in, it permeates all other layers. Living this way is nowhere near what we are capable of, nor does it allow us to access the resilience that is ours by nature.

I therefore encourage you to use your B.B.C. practice at every occasion, and when you feel ready, you can deepen your practice by including the following step, the Body Breath Mental Emotional freedom practice, which I call the B.B.M.E. It is an extended version of the B.B.C. and is just as easy to practise. It will reconnect you with your Inner Being, or core self. As you live closer to your source of power, your 'internal house' will be, once again, united.

Integrated Practical Awareness (I.P.A.)— Intermediate Practice

The following process, the Body Breath Mental Emotional (B.B.M.E.) practice, is another form of 'walking meditation', although, it can also be practised sitting down in stillness, in its more traditional form of regular meditation. The first time you practise it, you might like to keep your eyes closed, especially if you are not familiar with any form of meditation. In addition, you could record yourself on your phone while reading the exercise, so you can play it back as you learn the process. This will afford you an easier experience, and allow you to relax fully.[3]

Once you are familiar with the process, I encourage you to practise it with your eyes opened, while you walk around. This is really the aim of this process, which makes it particularly useful and adaptable to your daily activities, as you go about your day, drive the car, etc.

The following is the long version. If you find the whole process easy, or if you are used to meditating, a shorter version follows.

TOOL TWO—THE B.B.M.E. PRACTICE

Tuning in to Your B.B.M.E. (Body Breath Mental Emotional) Practice

- Start by using your B.B.C., which is to simply put your attention on your breath and to become aware of your feet making contact with the ground. Your breath may deepen as you become conscious of it, but let it happen naturally.

- Scan other parts of your body: your legs, your hips, your stomach, your solar plexus, your heart, your chest, your back, your neck and shoulders, your head, etc. Note if there is any tightness, discomfort or unease anywhere. You

---

[3] Visit me at www.drdugast.com to see online resources.

are not diagnosing, interpreting, analysing, or judging your findings. You are simply taking an inventory.

- Next, put your attention on your thoughts. Let's pretend that these thoughts are guests. By nature, you are peace; you don't need to find peace. Peace is already yours, right within you. All you have to do is to notice that your thoughts are layering what you already are by nature, which is peace. These thoughts are like 'guests' that are, for the most part, uninvited, repetitive, and, for the most part, less than positive. In fact, and because of a lack of supervision, these 'guests' have become thieves, stealing your peace of mind at will and you have allowed them to do so. At least, until today.

So right now, simply notice what thoughts are running your mind. Once again, you are simply taking an inventory. You might have a few thoughts, or many, it is not important right now. What is important is that you don't get into a conversation with these guests—your thoughts—as you usually do. You usually believe and entertain each and every one of them. There is constant noise, in the form of an internal conversation taking place, but not right now. Right now, you are simply taking an inventory, not engaging with any of them.

- Next, let's go to your emotions. We are going to use the same process as we did for the thoughts. Check in to see what kind of emotions are in you right now. These are also guests, and, for now, we are going to do the same thing: simply take an inventory, not engaging in analysing, magnifying, looking at the story that brought them here, etc. There are no right or wrong emotions; there are simply emotions. You may have one or more emotions going on within you at this time, some of which may be familiar ones. Some of these 'guests' are regular.

- While you observe what is going on in you, stay connected to your breathing.

- Now that you were able to note how your body feels, what kind of thoughts are in your mind, and what emotions you are feeling, it begs a question: who is doing the observing? The answer is: the consciousness, or source-part of you, which I call your 'Inner Being'. It is sometimes described as the witness, or the observer. All of them are fitting words to point toward this indescribable and non-physical part of us. Our Inner Being is a strange thing that we cannot look at, and yet, that we can look through, to gain insight. It is the part of us that is pristine, no matter what kind of damage our body, mind or emotions may have sustained. This Inner Being is pristine, untouched, perfect, and always there, awaiting our conscious decision to reconnect with it, by taking the focus off our usual mental-emotional involvement.

- Take three deep breaths to anchor this realisation. When you do, the contact with your Inner Being gets steadier, and it becomes easier and quicker to access. Another new habit. This will allow your own presence to radiate within you, and through you.

Note: Since it is an unseen part of us, this Inner Being is very often unacknowledged. We do not receive the education that it even exists, unless we develop an interest in personal development or metaphysical studies. This Inner Being can also be described as pure potential, as it is connected to the same Natural Intelligence that created anything that Man did not. It is the source of well-being, self-appreciation, self-healing, confidence, trust, regeneration, rejuvenation, and inspiration. It is the source from which the rest of our whole being, including all neurophysiological responses and processes are orchestrated with absolute precision.

Developing the habit of connecting to it with the two practices given so far means that you are adding conscious awareness to all your dealings and transactions. As already mentioned, it is your best and most powerful ally, and makes a great business partner! As you get used to accessing it, it will allow you to develop your intuition, which is your sense of knowing, beyond the five senses. This is a worthwhile attribute to develop, and an absolute asset for anyone who wants to gain awareness of what the physical eye cannot see. Because we live in a world of energy, and we can physically see very little, this will ensure that you have access to as much information as is available to you.

A Quicker Version of the B.B.M.E. Practice

Just like with the B.B.C., this is a practice you can use as you go about your day, and you can even use the same list of anchors. Simple events such as 'gaps' throughout the day, for example, waiting for an elevator, or going to the bathroom, provide perfect practice time. Here is a faster version of the B.B.M.E.:

- Take a breath, connect with your feet and the ground beneath them. This is your B.B.C.

- On the next breath, become aware of the rest of your body, and notice any unease or discomfort in any part of it. You are taking an inventory, not judging or analysing.

- Next, become aware of the thoughts in your mind. Do not engage with any of them, they are only guests. Simply take note, not judging or analysing.

- Next, become aware of the emotions within you at

this time. These too are guests. Do not indulge in any of them, simply take an inventory.

- Once you can do that, you are resting as your Inner Being, or conscious awareness. Take a deep breath to anchor this practice, and stay there as long as you wish, or as long as you can. This is the place where you can exist in absolute stillness. A place right within you, free from problems and constrictions.

ANCHORING YOUR STATE OF PEACE WITH A PHYSICAL GESTURE

The aim of selecting a physical gesture is to help you develop a physical habit from an internal state. I recommend that you do it, even if you don't feel any peace or any relief after you practised your B.B.M.E.

Choose a discreet physical gesture that you can do with only one of your hands, for discretion's sake. It must be something you can use easily at any time and in any circumstances, including if you had company and needed to keep your hand in your pocket. Every time you do it, you are teaching your physical body to anchor the mind-emotion respite being felt. Next time that you are faced with a stressful situation, your physical gesture may be the first thing to go into action, before you even think about using your B.B.M.E., particularly if you are a kinaesthetic[4] learner.

Soon enough, this new habit will become a learned, 'automatic' response. Think about when you first learned how to drive. Originally, you may have thought that it was hard, or that it took too much effort. But now you find it the easiest thing in the world. Although unfamiliar, both practices given so far, and the physical anchoring to go with it, are less complicated. The vehicle in question here is your own body, and your level of resilience and fulfilment depends on it. A small price to pay for incredible benefits! And you know what, this is far easier done than said!

Here Is the Full Sequence Put Together

- Practice your B.B.C. or the deeper practice of the B.B.M.E.

- When you feel even the slightest amount of peace, relief or well-being, use your chosen physical anchor to record this new state in your neurobiology. Do it if you don't feel anything too.

When the practices above have become habits, it means that your coping mechanism is at its best, able to

---

[4] Kinaesthetic learners absorb information by doing physical activities, like doodling and taking notes, rather than just listening or watching.

deal with anything that seemed previously difficult or stressful. Even if you feel a little stress, it won't last long. This is because your neurobiology, what I call your internal wiring, is set to respond differently. With complete resourcefulness, coming from your internal resourcefulness.

By then your resilience levels have increased substantially, and you can begin to enjoy a renewed sense of well-being, self-esteem and self-confidence.

9 Good Reasons to Tune in to Your B.B.M.E.

Tuning in to your B.B.M.E. is particularly useful when:

1. You think/feel that you might react negatively—verbally or physically—in a particular situation or conversation.

2. You have an overwhelming amount of dialogue going on in your mind.

3. You are at the mercy of your emotions, drowning in a familiar or recurrent state.

4. You cannot find sleep or any peace when trying to relax.

5. You feel that 'there is no way out' of your present situation or emotional state.

6. You feel you could do with an instant break or

holiday, but cannot take a physical break.

7. You need some instant self-confidence before a major decision, a meeting, public speaking, etc.

8. You need to access inspiration right in the moment, or get into your innovator/creator mode.

9. Things are going fantastically well, you are thriving AND you need to breathe it all in!

KNOW THYSELF—SO YOU CAN FREE THYSELF

Below is a diagram that depicts you. I am fond of humour and usually explain during an event, that, while you may think that this is not your 'best shot', it is, none the less, accurate.

You are the large circle that contains everything. You are the embodiment of what I call Natural Intelligence, which is a neutral name for the awesome force that created us. You are also the proud owner of three amazing attributes: your mind, your emotions and your physical body. Through the B.B.M.E. practice, you experienced yourself as conscious awareness, that I call your Inner Being, which is effectively being in contact with this Natural Intelligence. Before you even noticed resting as your Inner Being, you were perfectly able to take an inventory of what was going on in all three of your attributes: your body, your mind and your emotions. Please note the word *attributes*. This is a very important distinction. It means that, while you have great mental capacity at your disposal, a whole spectrum of possible emotions and a body, none of these are who you are at the core. This can free you as you read about it.

This also means these attributes no longer have the power to define you, as they are not who you are.

This can be a life-altering realisation as it means that what happened to you, if it was traumatic or even just upsetting, happened to one of your three attributes. The core part of you, your Inner Being, which is the essential part of you, remained untouched and even pristine. I like to call this Inner Being 'bulletproof', as it is resilience itself. Reading this can bring about instant and fundamental clearing of an old issue or concern that may have caused you pain or suffering until now. Please take a moment to observe the following diagram.

A Picture of You

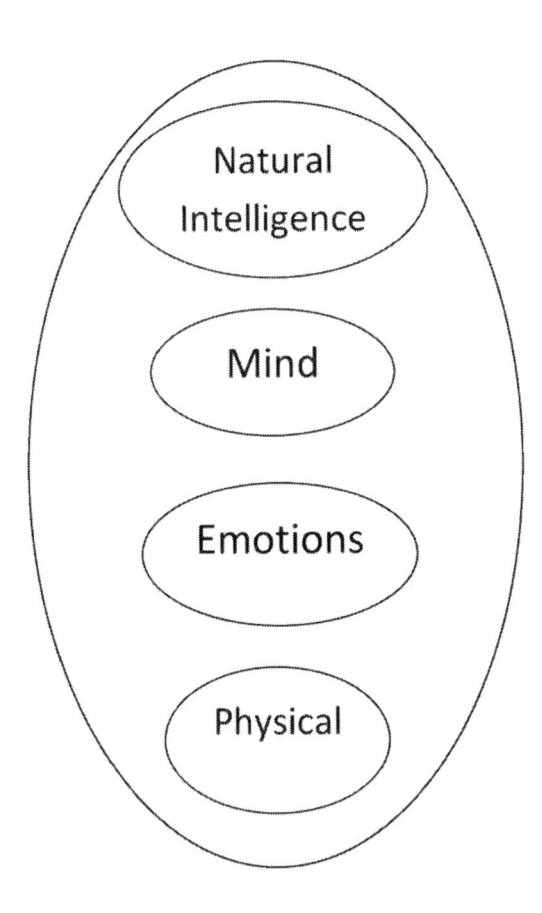

- Natural Intelligence
- Mind
- Emotions
- Physical

BUILDING RESILIENCE

Ending Years of Misconception and Pain

Thoughts and emotions left untamed are incredibly powerful, and can cause enough havoc to be devastating. The thought-emotion duo, which creates what we experience as *feelings*, can be as destructive or debilitating as it can be ultimately empowering. Feelings are at the base of the beliefs we hold as our reality. Unless you have access to the simple information you are reading here, this mind-emotion dynamic has the power to claim your full attention, draining you of much of your resources and energy. It will demand that you think and feel each thought and emotion as your identity, which couldn't be further from the truth.

René Descartes may have contributed to instilling the idea that we are our thoughts with his famous quote *"Cogito ergo sum" or "I think therefore I am"*. On one hand, this appeared revolutionary in the 1630s, and may have played a part in our evolution. On the other hand, it may very well have begun our accelerated descent into the abyss of the egotistical mind, which believes itself to be the sole proprietor of inspired or original thinking.

The fact is that, when the intellectual mind thinks it is all-ruling, it is reducing our awesome creative capacity to a lesser version of it, mainly based in control. This can spell boredom at the very least, or serious suffering. It also means that we miss a wealth of opportunities and information that is only accessible through accepting that we can access intelligence that is beyond the intellect, in the form of inspiration. The same information that is at the origin of all the *chef-d'oeuvre* and works of art ever produced. Absolutely everyone has access to this everlasting source of ideas and inspiration. It is only the 'mental noise', in the form of doubt, debates and arguments, that prevents it being heard.

We will study how to absolutely master our minds and have them work for us rather than our being subservient to them in the second part of this book. For now, we are preparing the grounds, so we no longer fall prey to the egotistical iron grip of the intellect. At least, not unless we want to make use of it.

In conclusion, we now know that we don't have to follow every thought that arises. Instead, we have a choice, which is to rest as conscious awareness, as our Inner Being, or, indeed, to harness our intellectual mind when the time to do so is appropriate, and not at 3 a.m. while trying to get to sleep.

Example: If John says 'I am depressed', it means that the 'I', his Inner Being, is depressed. This is not correct nor true or even possible. The trouble is that we feel every thought we think, and we end up thinking every feeling we have. Because of the internal creative process, as is outlined in the diagram, thoughts and emotions define the steps and the decisions we make. Someone who is depressed might stay in bed, or watch TV all day, feeling that going out or reaching out is too much.

Now that John knows about the two steps we have just studied, he could say, 'There is depression in me right now', which is very different from identifying as depression itself. It leaves a gap, however small, that can allow him to practice his B.B.M.E. as one part of him is not tied to the depression.

While this may look like a small shift, it can provide a breakthrough. It actually means that this state of depression, which can happen to any of us, is a passing state. This will allow it to not become a chronic, emotional illness. It allows John to have access to his inner resources, which he will certainly benefit from as he practices his B.B.M.E. Remember that this, too, is cumulative.

Holding on tight to any positive emotions would also be the same. There may be joy, happiness, excitement, sadness, or any of the many emotions we have access to as human beings. Reconnecting with your Inner Being will allow you to not be attached to any of them, but instead, enjoy freedom as they will not have a hold on you. In fact, as you practise the two simple steps given so far, you will get used to feeling a growing sense of 'inner security'. The kind of internal support and instant relief that comes from connecting with your innermost resources, your Inner Being. This will certainly allow you to develop a steady and powerful sense of gratitude that will permeate even the toughest of emotional states. While these may arise, they will be vaporised by gratitude and peace.

Labelling Yourself Is Powerful: Choose Carefully

Aside from making a mental or an emotional state permanent, labelling yourself with certain emotions is a dangerous thing to do, particularly if they are a low frequency emotion. This is because language is a frequency in itself, and has far more momentum than you can imagine. Words literally are the carrier of energy, so to keep on declaring yourself as poor, depressed, unsuccessful, or unable to do this or that depletes your confidence further. This creates a self-perpetuating loop, as your mind will keep recreating images and situations that can confirm your choice. If you want to label yourself, you could choose, 'lucky', 'resourceful', 'resilient', or any other words that can actually carry a frequency that can help you.

Encrypted Wisdom

I have lived in Ireland for 21 years, and although I can, by no means, speak its beautiful, ancient Celtic language, I know enough to know that like many other ancient languages, it is encrypted with truth. For example, '*Is ocras orm*' means 'I am hungry'. But the accurate translation for this is 'Hunger is upon me', which wonderfully illustrates what we have just studied.

Please take a moment to let the diagram above seep into you, especially if your learning style is visual. If you are a kinaesthetic learner, you might even like to draw it for yourself. It will help your mind to begin forming new neural pathways, as it absorbs this information and literally creates new possibilities. The point is that mind, emotions and physical body are not who you are, but instead, they are your attributes. They will work with you, if you know how to handle them.

This simple diagram also serves well to illustrate the famous declaration of independence:

"All men are created equal."

As you read these words, let right now be your own declaration of independence. Freedom, abundance, ultimate resilience, and independence—from which comes freedom—begin with information. Information can then be transmuted into wisdom. This will be more and more readily accessible as you choose to use your B.B.C. and/or the B.B.M.E. steps.

Practise makes permanent; nobody is looking for 'perfect'. There is no such thing as perfection, other than this moment just as it is, and you, accepting yourself exactly as you are.

Case Study—Henry

Someone I will call Henry was one among many who lost his job in 2008. To add to this, he also lost his lifetime savings. Determined to turn things around, he borrowed some money from his family and a few close friends, to keep up his mortgage repayments, and to fund an idea for a new business. He worked extraordinarily hard to make sure it would take off, but unfortunately, the business did not make it. It was only a short, few months later that the family home was repossessed, which is when Henry sank into deep depression. His self-worth plummeted down, along with his close, personal relationships. His wife and four children relocated to live with his wife's mother, leaving little chance for their marriage to survive. This heralded an all-time low for Henry, as everything he identified as parts of himself disappeared from his life in a few short months. He seriously considered taking his own life on several occasions. He felt completely empty and bereft.

When I met Henry, he had the look of a man who was expecting to wake from his nightmare any second. He was cynical, and did not start using the practices given because he believed that they might work, but simply because he had nothing left to lose.

As he quickly learnt to rest as his core self, or Inner Being, he got regular breaks from the perception that said he lost his identity. With a little more practise, his own sense of awareness shifted and, with it, his whole reality. He began to experience a kind of inner strength he had not previously known. As this grew a little each day, he got some self-confidence back, and before long, he decided to take a job, any job, to begin rebuilding his life and his prospects.

By the time he was able to use the full process—NeuroBiology Reprogramming™—he was able to clear some beliefs and long-held limitations that he hadn't been aware of, as most of these were unconscious. He was able to clear years of limitations. He also took immense comfort in realising that his last business idea had not been a bad one, but that he simply did not have the resilience to see it through, due to some beliefs he took on board.

The story ends very well for Henry. Today, he is a successful entrepreneur. As he won the game of life and the game of business, he also won his wife's heart back. His family is extraordinarily united, and he admits that if he could go back in the past and do it any other way, he wouldn't. He says that he has never felt so alive, so fulfilled and so grateful as he does today, and that he probably wouldn't have realised all of this unless he had gone through this life-altering crisis. It isn't that challenges have stopped, quite the contrary, success brings its own challenges. He simply has tools, uses them, and knows how to handle them, one at a time, and always from the inside out.

The good news for you reading this is that you don't need to wait until you lose anything. You can benefit from the same breakthrough by simply applying the steps included here. We have just studied two, and, altogether, there are only three. Life is good!

THE WEALTH FACTOR

Because our thoughts are at the top of our manifesting ability, which we will see in detail in the coming chapters, and because they have energy and tremendous momentum, we become what we think about repeatedly. This means that everything is possible, from stress-based illness, poverty and loneliness, all the way to success and abundance in all things. Once we know how this works, the choice is ours. We have enough free will to stay stuck, or get free, and have fun creating a life that reflects our potential.

As you practise tuning in to your B.B.M.E., remaining conscious and resourceful become habits. A less burdened mind, one that knows peace, can receive inspired ideas and solutions that can resolve the situation at hand. Nothing of any value can come to a mind filled with fear and self-deprecating thoughts. Inspiration, which is effectively inner direction, needs internal spaciousness to be perceived. The ability to step back as conscious awareness—as your Inner Being—is the most precious resource you can access. This is the kind of wealth that cannot be bought. This inner wealth is the foundation, the basis for all other kinds of successes such as joy, gratitude, boundless energy, inspired ideas, well-being, extraordinary relationships, and last but not least, ideas and alliances that can produce material wealth.

Anything you are looking to create or sustain in tangible terms must be an internal state first. Success is always an inside job first.

LET'S TALK STORY!

This Is a Short Story: A Hybrid Between Tolstoy and an Ancient Indian Fable

Once upon a time, there was a beggar. He was found exhausted and starving, sitting outside the temple. The villagers took care of him, gave him water, food and shelter.

This beggar sat out on the streets every day, pleading for pennies from passers-by. He was so caught up in the doom and gloom of his self-inflicted notion of poverty that he failed to notice that the pot on which he was sitting each day was in fact a glimmering pot of gold.

The villagers found the pot after the beggar died. They used the gold coins to renovate the temple.

CHAPTER 2—PRACTICE RECAP 1

Integrated Practical Awareness
I.P.A.—INTERMEDIATE PRACTICE

TOOL TWO: Tuning in to your B.B.M.E.

1. Put your attention on your feet and notice your breathing. Feel your feet on the ground; this is your B.B.C.

2. Become aware of your physical body. You are taking an inventory, not judging or evaluating.

3. Now pay attention to your thoughts. You are still taking an inventory; you are not entertaining or following any of them.

4. Next, notice the emotions that are in you right now. Do not analyse them or engage with them. You are simply taking an inventory.

5. Once you can observe all that is going on within you, you are resting as your Inner Being. Take 3 deep breaths to anchor this practice. You are teaching your neurobiology a new response.

CHAPTER 2—PRACTICE RECAP 2

Integrated Practical Awareness
I.P.A.—INTERMEDIATE PRACTICE

ADDING A PHYSICAL ANCHOR

1. Select a physical gesture that is easy and discreet.

2. Use it following each time that you have used your B.B.M.E. practice to teach your mind-emotions—your neurobiology—a new response.

Note: You can use the same list of reminders as you drew up for your B.B.C. This will help you remember to practise as often as possible.

CHAPTER 3

INTEGRATED PRACTICAL AWARENESS

I.P.A. LEVEL III: ADVANCED PRACTICE

RECLAIMING YOUR POWER

*"Many people are alive
but don't touch the miracle of being alive."*

— Thich Nhat Hanh

RECLAIMING YOUR POWER

You have just had an experience of who you really are at the core with the practice of B.B.M.E. Your success now lies in the practise. Be kind to yourself, as developing any kind of new practice can take time. Just like you wouldn't expect your muscles to be fully toned following a handful of workouts at the gym, your 'consciousness muscle' will also require some time to develop. Beyond this, it will take some repeated practise so it can become a habit. When it does, you will begin to feel quite free, as this will have become your first response.

In the last chapter, we began to answer an age-old question: 'Who am I?' Understanding who you are and how you function will in itself answer many of your queries in terms of why some things may not have worked out until now. It will make taking care of your own internal wiring clearer and more relevant, as you will gradually appreciate that you really do have more control in how you create your life; at least, in the choices you make and how you respond.

The following exercise will help you to begin clearing some old beliefs that you may still be carrying inadvertently, as these are lodged in the subconscious mind. These beliefs play a huge part in how you feel about yourself, as they affect your level of resilience and therefore what choices and opportunities are available to you. As you free yourself from influences you took on board, you will effectively be able to reclaim parts of you. You may also experience a boost of energy, as you are no longer burdened by extraneous, cumbersome and reductional beliefs. Completing the exercise will have the effect of a good 'spring clean', and you will be able to recollect pieces of you that have been scattered across space and time.

EXERCISE
Personal Inventory

Four Things You Are NOT

To get a clearer understanding of who you are, and to reclaim your full power, it is helpful to go through a process of elimination, to recognise what you are not. Here are four things you are not:

- Your past circumstances,
- Your present circumstances,
- Other people's opinions, and
- Your own inner critic.

There is a great deal more that we hold as beliefs than the three examples given in each section, so take these as suggestions to begin the work of self-inquiry. You can absolutely add to each exercise to see where else you might have left parts of you.

1) **Past circumstances:** Name 1-3, or more, things that have held you back until today.

Please note that the beginning of these phrases are only examples, you can write your own.

If I had ……….. (done otherwise), by now, I could have ……………………………………………………. (achieved or created something I really wanted to do).

If……………… (someone you know) didn't …………………………………… (say or do something to me), I could have…………………………. (done something I really wanted to do).

If …………………. (some external circumstances) hadn't happened, I might be able to ………………… (find a solution or realise a goal).

2) **Present circumstances:** Name 1-3 things that are holding you up right now.

If I had more .... (time, money, skills, etc.), I could ....

When............................ (something happens in the future), I will be able to .... (do, be or have what I really want to experience).

I will be happy/at peace when .... (something you are waiting for in the future).

3) **Other people's opinion:** Name 1-3 limiting beliefs that you have accepted from someone else.

I am not good at .... (something you have been telling yourself, based on a judgement someone made about you at some point).

I was told that...

.... and until now, I believed it.

I remember .... (a parent, a lover, a sibling, a teacher, a friend) saying that I was not .... enough.

4) **Your own inner critic, which can effectively be called your inner bully:** Name 1-3 things you tell yourself often, that are limiting in essence.

I am not enough/not lovable enough because...............

....

If I wasn't so...................................., I could......

....

When I ...., I will be able to ....

How Did You Get On?

You may have encountered some excuses, regrets, some blame, and some limits you accepted as permanent truths, when, in fact, these are someone else's opinion. Some are so deeply engrained in you that you think of them as your own identity, never doubting or even questioning any of them. Such are some of the subconscious limits that keep the lid shut on your potential. Most or all of these would remain undetected, unquestioned, unless you used the power of self-inquiry.

- Take this opportunity to use your B.B.C. and get a moment's respite, as you feel a little freer. You deserve it.

- On your next inhalation, breathe through your body, past your thoughts and emotions, using your B.B.M.E. practice. On the exhale, you can release all that you put down on paper in this exercise. On your next inhalation, breathe straight to your core, your Inner Being, to refuel on well-being and appreciate that all is well, and getting better as we journey together.

- Use your physical gesture to anchor this state of well-being, freedom and peace.

LET'S TALK STORY!

A Sufi Story About the Great Nasruddin

Nasruddin Hodja was lying in the shade of an ancient walnut tree. His body was at rest, but, befitting his calling as an imam, his mind did not relax. Looking up into the mighty tree he considered the greatness and wisdom of Allah.

'Allah is great and Allah is good,' said the Hodja, 'but was it indeed wise that such a great tree as this be created to bear only tiny walnuts as fruits? Behold the stout stem and strong limbs. They could easily carry the great pumpkins that grow from spindly vines in yonder field, vines that cannot begin to bear the weight of their own fruit. Should not walnuts grow on weakly vines and pumpkins on sturdy trees?'

So thinking, the Hodja dozed off, only to be awakened by a walnut that fell from the tree, striking him on his forehead.

'Allah be praised!' he exclaimed, seeing what had happened. 'If that had been a pumpkin that fell on my head, it would have killed me for sure! Allah is merciful! He has rearranged nature only to spare my life.'

CHAPTER 3—PRACTICE RECAP

Integrated Practical Awareness
I.P.A.—ADVANCED PRACTICE

RECLAIMING YOUR OWN POWER

Personal inventory exercise - Four things you are not:

1) Past circumstances
2) Present circumstances
3) Other people's opinions
4) Your own inner critic

CHAPTER 4

TIME RESILIENCE

"The timeless in you is aware of life's timelessness. And knows that yesterday is but today's memory and tomorrow is today's dream."

— Kahlil Gibran

WHAT TIME IS IT?

In textbook dictionaries, time is defined as 'a progress in existence', or 'a measure in which events can be ordered from the past through the present into the future'. While all of these are fitting descriptions for daily functioning and organising, in reality, time is just a concept. Depending on the nature of the moment you are experiencing and the feelings associated with it, the same amount of time can be experienced as a fleeting moment, or as an endless, unbearable ordeal.

For example, if you have a broken leg and are waiting to be rescued, each minute that passes will seem like hours. Whereas if you are spending time with your beloved, or watching your favourite sport, hours will seem like minutes. We therefore cannot look at the nature of time without looking at the nature of the mind, and its effect on the emotional body, for these three elements are closely intertwined. Therefore, your mindset and the feelings associated with it largely influence our perception of the passing moment.

You Are a Time-Traveller

As human beings, we are the only species on the planet that has the amazing capacity to create from a single idea, using our mind. We can literally think something up, and go about to create it in tangible terms. Ideas are one of our most valuable currencies, as they literally represent the 'seed of creation'. Take a look around you right now. Anything you can set your eyes on is the product of one of two creative forces: it is either man-made or Natural Intelligence-made (you can call this God-made if you are easy with spiritual terms). We have the awesome privilege of having access to one of these two incredible forces. Think about that for a minute. This is absolutely amazing as it literally determines the nature of our reality. I am not throwing this out as a pie-in-the-sky concept, suggesting that 'wishful thinking will get you what you want'. Instead, we will break down piece by piece how you can do this, and make the necessary adjustments so you can begin to create on purpose rather than by default.

Most of the time, or until we have enough self-discipline, we use this immense creative power against ourselves. We mentally replay events that have happened in the past, with which we create a probable future. Why would anyone do that? Absolutely no good reason, at least, not once we understand how this works. We have just had a small taste in freeing your potential with the exercise you did in the last chapter, and there is much more to come, with which you will be able to literally liberate your own creative energy.

It is surprising to see that even when we know about this, how we use this ability does not reflect anywhere near even a fraction of our human potential, because much of what we think is fear-based in nature, and all of it is in subconscious mode. If you'll simply pay attention to your thoughts, see how long you can go without thinking something that has to do with fear, self-doubt, self-hatred, or worry ... you'll then see what I mean.

We primarily use one part of our mind: the conscious mind and mainly for one purpose, which is to indulge in these kinds of 'programmed thoughts', beliefs such as I have just mentioned. The conscious mind is actually the only part of the mind that can travel through time, back and forth. This is like having a fantastic asset with no idea how to use it, which is why it creates a lot more problems and challenges than it ought to. This is literally the only part of our intricate human mechanism that can time-travel. So when we choose to keep running on fear-based thinking, even though much of it may be unconscious, it literally becomes a self-fulfilling prophecy. This is what divides our power, and is at the root of all our problems, including our lack of resilience, which limits our abundance in all things. It is a bit like being thrown into a Rolls Royce car at high speed (or a Porsche, if you prefer!) and having no idea how to drive it.

Thoughts, both conscious and unconscious, are the sources of emotions, and emotions very much determine what actions we take. Any thought that is steeped in fear will incur a reaction rather than a conscious action. The challenge is, as many great historical leaders said it, and as uncle Ben mentioned it to Peter Parker, a.k.a. Spiderman:

"With great power comes great responsibility."

The ability to co-create our reality is such a

responsibility. First comes knowledge and the realisation of how we really function, and how we contribute to our own life and our environment. Then comes the choice to develop enough self-discipline using the tools given to steer ourselves in the direction of success. Better still if our choices do not deplete anything or anyone along the way. Then we can create results that can almost feel like 'miracles', big and small.

How History Repeats Itself

From a simple thought, the memory of an event that happened in the past can be 're-lit' and influence our whole biochemistry with the same emotional charge again.

Until trained, the mind-emotion attributes run all our dealings. We are not in control of our mind, but our mind, or the information in it, is in control of us. Most stories about why someone is not where they really want to be today—whether in health, business or relationship—is because they are tied to the memory of a past event or situation. Such is the power of the mind, and this is precisely how history repeats itself.

The mind can effectively be described either as a liability or an asset. It is a liability when it is left to run riot, untrained and untamed, allowed to anticipate the worst probable future based on past events. Not only does using the mind this way ruin the vast potential that is available in the moment, it also prohibits peace of mind, self-confidence, and drains every bit of resilience we may have. This is how the same results are recreated endlessly.

'Worry', for example, is a common, fear-based practice that most people engage in daily. Worry can be accurately described as praying for things to go wrong, or making sure that we energise the worst possible outcomes. It perpetrates a life that is constantly trapped between escaping imagined negative events and surviving ordeals. And this doesn't just stay in the mind, it means that our neurochemistry runs on stress and sustains the fight-or-flight state every day, all day. This provides the perfect ground for physical illness.

Yet, there is much that is available to us once we have a handle on our conscious mind. We can begin to create from trust and confidence, regain a sense of peace, and literally put an end to history repeating itself. This is completely within your power.

A simple example: Let's say that Jenny is driving home from work. While she always looks forward to seeing her spouse and children, she finds that this feeling almost never carries over. As she drives home, she usually finds herself replaying events from her day at work. Right now, her mind jumps to an altercation that happened earlier in the day with a colleague at work, Bob. As she goes over the event again, she begins to feel anger rise in her, and by the time another car cuts across her, she is feeling irate. She carries on driving, planning what she will say to Bob at work tomorrow. By the time she walks in the door, she is tired and angry, and her mind is still in the grip of what happened earlier on, and how she will react tomorrow. When she sees her spouse and children, she feels preoccupied, and no longer feels the positive anticipation that she did earlier on. She let her conscious mind travel back to her day's work, which set up a whole chain reaction of emotions, and she ends up taking out her mood on the people she loves the most.

What Could Have Jenny Done?

This is a very common scenario that can be very easily transformed with a single decision. Jenny could have used her B.B.C. step earlier on in the day, during the altercation with Bob. While driving home, which provides the perfect setting to 'regroup' and have time to herself, she could use her B.B.M.E. step. If she still felt too much leftover 'mind-emotion pollution' from the day, once she parked the car, she could have taken a couple of minutes, time enough to close her eyes and take 2-3 more deep and relaxing breaths, to get reconnected to her source of well-being. This is incredibly simple, and it would have helped her to leave the day—and the events—behind, and come into the family home in full presence, with a smile, bringing in what she intended, which was joy and positive anticipation.

EXERCISE—PART 1
Where Do You Live?

Look at the following diagrams, and take a moment to identify where you spend most of your mind-time.

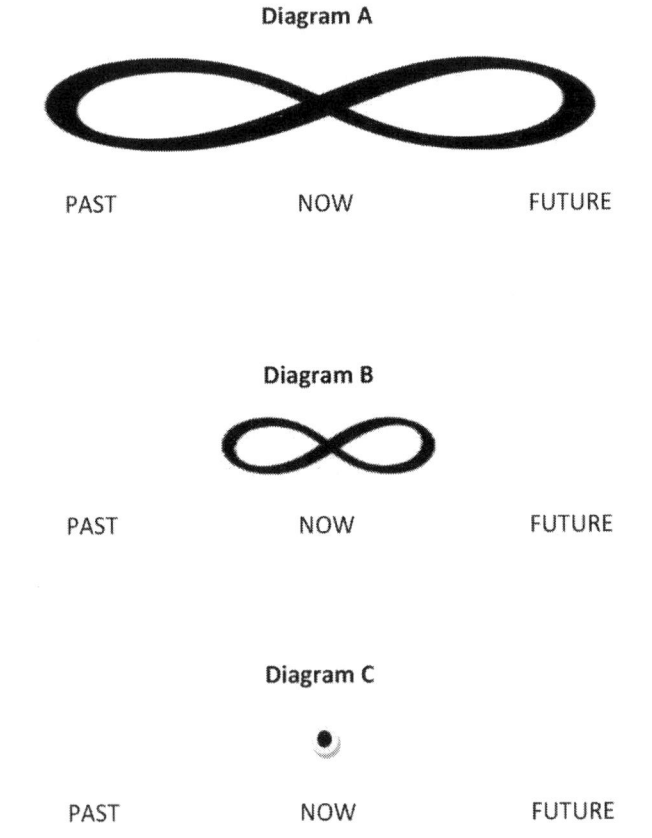

Diagram A

PAST　　　　　NOW　　　　　FUTURE

Diagram B

PAST　　　　　NOW　　　　　FUTURE

Diagram C

PAST　　　　　NOW　　　　　FUTURE

Diagram A depicts the mind spending most of its time in the past and the future. This illustrates the mind of someone who is completely at the mercy of their mind, with no knowledge or discipline on how to use it. Rather, they are run by their own mind and the thoughts in it, and very much at the mercy of it. The figure of eight lying down—also known as a lemniscate, or infinity symbol—extends back and forth, creating, what I call, in this particular context, a 'crazy loop'. This is the worst case scenario, with the person never able to rest in the present moment—the now—the only place of power, resilience and influence. Tremendous suffering and ultimate limitations rule this kind of mind.

Diagram B depicts a mind that is slightly more disciplined, and is allowed to spend less time in the past and the future. This person knows how to come back to the present moment, and therefore enjoys respite from the tyrannical influence from the mind, and can feel an amount of peace. Creative power can be harnessed at times, and be used to see goals and plans to completion.

Diagram C depicts a mind that is most disciplined. This person can enjoy being in the present moment at will, using self-discipline. The 'crazy-loop' is no more, or if it arises, doesn't last very long. Travelling back in the past or forward into the future may be applied purposefully, and whenever required, to analyse past mistakes or to actualise plans and goals, using personal vision and foresight. This is someone who avails of peace of mind at will, and can make use of their higher mind—Natural Intelligence—at will.

Please tick the appropriate. "I spend of most of my mind-time as depicted in":

- Diagram A
- Diagram B
- Diagram C

Once you have evaluated where you spent most of your time until today—if not fully present most of the time—the good news is that now you know you can choose differently.

EXERCISE—PART 2
Mastering Time and Preparing for Mental Resilience

You will feel a substantial amount of mental resilience when you can control its time-travelling capacity. Using the anchors you chose earlier on, including your daily irritants and your joy-filled factors, will ensure that your B.B.C. and/or your B.B.M.E. practice is ongoing. Using your physical gesture upon practising either or both steps gives you a tangible anchor, and allows for your neurobiology to have a completely different response to life's events and stresses.

As you make different choices, you will get a sense of how you spend your time, and regain the ability to enjoy each passing moment. Time is our most precious currency, once it is gone, it cannot be gained back.

The quality of your life depends on your appreciation of each passing moment. Gratitude is one of the best and fastest thought-forms when it comes to feeling instantly better. It will ensure that you feel you are making the most of your life with each of your choices and commitments.

The following phrases are designed to tie together all the exercises we have done until now, so their practice and effect can be crystal clear in your mind.

Tying Up the Full I.P.A. Practical Awareness

Please read the following, and fill in the blanks.

"From now on, I decide to harness my own power by choosing to come back to the present moment as often as possible, using my B.B.C.

When I feel in the grip of my mind-emotions and experience difficulties in being connected to my inner resources—my Inner Being—I choose to help myself and to practise my B.B.M.E., which is a deeper version of the B.B.C.

In times of need or stress, I can practise the B.B.M.E. with my eyes closed for a deeper experience, as this is a simple way to meditate.

I am committed to using .... (my daily irritants) and .... (the things that delight me) as my cues to remember to practise either or both steps as often as possible.

This is a win-win scenario, as no matter what happens, I can use any event to reconnect to my ultimate resources, and access the resilience that is already within me. This will grow a little more with each practice.

Every time I practise the B.B.C. and/or the B.B.M.E., I will use my chosen physical anchor, which is ....

This simple practice allows me to naturally rewire my own neurobiology, and teach my body-mind a different response to all my dealings and life events.

This means that I am creating new neural pathways in my mind, opening the space for success in my life, and literally carving a new destiny for myself.

I feel immensely grateful right now, to be here, learning how to use the most powerful tools to finally actualise my heart's deepest desire.

This is what I have been waiting for and I was able to take the first step by reading this book. I am grateful to my own sense of guidance, and I know that I am always in the right place at the right time."

Q&A

These questions and answers are taken from live and online events.

Q: Is revisiting the past ever a good idea?

A: It is sometimes very useful, particularly if used to identify, for example, what went wrong—or what was great—in a project or a business. It is just like doing a project or business 'autopsy'. Very important in business, especially if you are a leader/entrepreneur, a solo-preneur or in a partnership.

It will be even more pertinent if you can see clearly enough to identify how you contributed personally. When you have the clarity and foresight to recognise your own mindset, and how it contributed to what happened, you are able to make new grounds. Remember that success is always 'an inside job' first. Taking responsibility means that you are taking your full power back.

A word of caution, however, which is to stay away from blame, no matter the findings. Whether anyone may be tempted to direct blame toward self or someone else, it is ultimately useless, time wasting, and energy depleting, particularly for the one doing the blaming. Blaming means giving our power away. The truth is that when we know better, we do better. We cannot redo something that happened in the past. Rather, we can use the gift of increased consciousness and make new grounds, so we can move forward. As with most self-realising exercises, making amends is at its most powerful when it begins with self. This is the ability to forgive. For giving ourselves the peace that is ours by nature. So yes, forgiving yourself, and others, is an important part of building future success, which can only happen in the moment, one minute at a time, free from the burden of the past. You are, no doubt, familiar with one of Albert Einstein's most popular quotes:

"Insanity: doing the same thing over and over again and expecting different results."

Q: When is revisiting the past not a good thing to do?

A: In short, when it is causing you pain, or when nothing productive can come out of revisiting it. For example, replaying an event that caused stress and pain in either mental, emotional and physical attributes will have no good outcome. The best course of action in this case is to use the replaying event in the same way that we use the 'daily irritants': your reminder to practise your steps. When you can think of a past event without any emotional charge, it means that have gained wisdom. Using your B.B.M.E. steps will help you to forgive and let go. If being stuck in regret, grief, anger, or resentment is holding up your own success, take your power back now.

Until now, you may have felt like a victim, unable to escape invading thoughts replaying, not realising that each time this happened, you really gave your power away. Now you know that the same thoughts are in fact your ally, reminding you to use your B.B.C. and/or your B.B.M.E.; you can see that no matter what happens, life works in your favour. Isn't that wonderful? No matter the reason you are here today, you are the beneficiary as your consciousness grows, and you are learning to get free, to reclaim your full power and ultimate resilience. This wouldn't have happened unless you went through what you did. There is so much to be grateful for, and remember, gratitude is the fastest and most transformative mind-emotion energy you can behold.

Q: Is projecting oneself in the future a good idea?

A: Yes, sometimes, depending on why you do it, and how you use what you see. As mentioned earlier on, if you are anticipating a future situation to be like a past one, and if the anticipation is of a negative nature, you are paving the way for 'failure'. If you are anticipating a future event to be like a positive or successful past event, you are still limiting the extent of what is possible. Remember that the nature of reality is ever changing, and being attached to wanting the same results is always limiting.

The best use of your 'time-travelling' mind ability is to use it the way innovators, visionaries, thinkers, leaders, strategists, planners, authors, script writers, etc. make use of it. This means that a vision or an idea is the fuel to manifesting something in the present. An important distinction is make sure you take a physical step in the moment, upon receiving an inspired idea. Otherwise, these ideas remain in the realm of wishful thinking, which will not bear any results. Taking massive action is a step often missed. While this may sound like common sense, it is often disregarded and many ideas remain just that: ideas, or 'pies in the sky'. You are here, in the body, which is a great tool with which you can experience and design a reality that you want to experience. Make use of it, it is a gift!

Q: With financial and business success in mind, is focusing on thinking in the present moment ever a good idea?

A: Let me make sure you know that you can give yourself a break from thinking before I say anything else. Your mind is one of your three attributes, and not who you are at the core. This will afford much 'mental flexibility'.

Having said that, intellectual thinking is, of course, a powerful tool, especially if free from all other concerns. This is when it is at its most powerful. An excellent habit, given to me by a millionaire acquaintance, is to create a designated space, and allocate an amount of time each day to engage in strategic thinking. This is particularly useful if you intend on being very successful, are already successful and would like to be even more so.

A large part of success relies on being organised. Strategic thinking can certainly give you the clarity and the means to create a plan for what has to be done, and to divide it into a workable format. Some things have to be done monthly, others weekly, and having a daily plan is of the essence. Even better if it was prepared the evening before.

Starting each day with a crystal clear idea of what to do makes all the difference, rather than fumbling around hoping to get as much done as possible. These decisions and actions are precisely what keeps overload or overwhelm from taking over. As you learn to take better care of yourself, you naturally look for ways to avoid stress-filled situations. You could say that strategic thinking and forward planning are external manifestations of internal peace of mind. There is great peace of mind in being organised. It can afford you some thinking space and, in turn, some peace of mind! So yes, focusing on thinking in the present moment can be invaluable.

LET'S TALK STORY!

Adapted from a Well-Known Zen Story

Two Buddhist Monks were on a pilgrimage, one was a senior monk; the other, a junior monk. During their journey they approached a raging river. On the river bank stood a young lady, weeping. She was frightened of the water and sat there, helpless, unable to cross over.

The junior monk walked straight past her without giving her a thought, and crossed the river without looking back.

The senior monk picked up the woman, carried her across the river and placed her down. They parted ways.

Toward the end of the day, the young monk could hold it no longer. 'How could you carry her like that? You know we can't touch women; it's against our way of life!'

The senior monk looked at him, and quietly added, 'I left the woman at the river's edge many hours ago; why are you still carrying her?'

CHAPTER 4—PRACTICE RECAP

TIME RESILIENCE

EXERCISE—PART 1: Where Do You Live?

Seeing where you spend most of your mind-time and learning to situate yourself in the present moment, for maximum efficiency and peace of mind.

EXERCISE—PART 2: Mastering Time and Preparing for Mental Resilience

Tying your whole Integrated Practical Awareness sequence together. Read the phrases given to consolidate your practice so far: your B.B.C. and your B.B.M.E. steps, followed by anchoring it with your physical gesture.

This is all you need to do to learn a new habit, and let your neurobiology be rewired to have a completely different response to life's events.

PART ONE—FULL PRACTICE RECAP

I.P.A. Integrated Practical Awareness

A Summary of the 2 STEPS Given So Far

STEP 1: When you feel stressed or joyful, take a breath in and feel your feet on the ground: **This is your first step, your B.B.C. practice.**

STEP 2: When you feel at the mercy of your mind-emotion, use your B.B.C. and deepen it by noting—but not engaging with—your thoughts and emotions. This will allow you to experience yourself as conscious awareness, as your Inner Being, the part of you where all is always well: **This is your B.B.M.E. practice.**

To remember to practise either step, use your daily anchors: **Your daily irritants and/or the things that delight you.**

Upon practising either or both step(s), link your new state of peace with your chosen physical gesture.

You are allowing your own neurobiology to begin reprogramming itself:
Ultimate resilience is yours!

PART TWO

NEUROBIOLOGY REPROGRAMMING™

N.B.R. Level ONE: MENTAL RESILIENCE

N.B.R. Level TWO: EMOTIONAL RESILIENCE

N.B.R. Level THREE: PHYSICAL RESILIENCE

"Awareness by itself is not enough: it must be joined by mastery. We need gradually to develop a steering ability to keep ourselves from slipping mechanically into this or that sub-personality. Thus we become able to identify with each part of our being as we wish. We can have more choice. It is the difference between being impotently transported by a roller coaster and, instead, driving a car and being able to choose which way to go and for what purpose to make the journey."

— Piero Ferrucci

CHAPTER 5

NEUROBIOLOGY REPROGRAMMING™

LEVEL ONE: MENTAL RESILIENCE

"The beginning of wisdom is the definition of terms."
— Socrates

Connecting the DOTS™

Whether you have been a mindfulness practitioner prior to reading this book or have just begun to apply your B.B.C. and B.B.M.E. steps, you might wonder if being aware is enough. This is a very valid question. Another useful self-reflecting question is 'Can I really create the kind of results or the quality of life I have in mind by simply being aware?', or 'As an entrepreneur, does awareness make me resilient enough to keep trying, to keep rebuilding past the many failed attempts that naturally occur on the path to creating something stable, something extraordinary?', or 'Does greater awareness alone give me the tools to navigate away from hereditary patterns and limiting beliefs?'

When I asked myself these questions, and even though it came after more than 25 years of practicing mindfulness, I found that the answer to them all was a definite 'no'. While this may appear controversial to anyone practising mindfulness for a number of years, it deeply resonated with me. I realised something simple, which is that it takes many 'bricks' to build a house. As we get more aware, there is more *insight*, more clarity available to us. We can better see what is outmoded in our own thinking, our own behaviour, and how these contribute to our personal and professional life, including how we contribute to others.

A glass window looks quite clean when it is not too brightly lit, but as more light shines on it, all the watermarks show up.

Due to repeating stumbling blocks, I asked myself why such challenges kept on replaying in my life. As I did, I came to the evident conclusion that the common denominator, consistent throughout anything that I ever got involved with—and no matter how far back I looked—was none other than me. With this realisation came two choices.

One: to keep blaming external circumstances, people and events and feeling like a victim. This choice is perpetrated by expressions in our choice of thoughts and language such as 'Why me?' or 'Why does this keep on happening?', which is depleting, limited and completely disempowering.

Two: taking responsibility and seeing what can be done that is within our own power. This puts us back in the driver's seat, affording us to take ownership and full responsibility. It means that we can do what it takes to transform what doesn't work, so we can create what we want to experience.

The second choice allowed me to seek and find the next piece of the human-potential puzzle, and to insure the transformation of even the most invisible or long-standing subconscious patterns. This allowed me to connect my own dots, and create seminars carrying the same name: Connecting the DOTS™.

Are We Responsible for Everything That Happens to Us?

Everyone creates according to their mindset, whether they know it or not. This means that there is much that is outside our control. However, our reactions are our own, and so is what we make out of any situation with which we are involved. This choice is valid for us all. Whether the challenges we experience are repetitive, or are isolated occurrences, they are here for a reason. We can even say that they are a gift.

Some challenges are healthy, demanding that we grow beyond the occasion, and others are simply repeating ordeals that need to be transformed, to make room for the new. Both kinds of challenges will demand that we shift our mindset, which is made considerably easier by understanding how our mind really functions. This is where 'Know Thyself' comes in handy and is important, as it gives us essential clues to 'crack our own human coding'. There are fewer investments we could engage in that have the power to yield as many dividends as our own personal development. Any really successful person knows that. Knowing ourselves is precisely how we can get to know the world, for this is exactly the way reality operates: from the inside out. Investing in our own development is like making sure we understand the rules of the game, so we can actually win it! Because anything we can create begins in the mind, so if we understand it, we are halfway there. The other half comes from practising what we know. Both combined means that you can certainly win this game.

THE NATURE AND PURPOSE OF THE MIND

The mind is Man's most powerful attribute. It runs on the fastest kind of 'fuel' we have access to: thought-forms, which we perceive as ideas. Ideas are one of our most precious currencies as they are at the root of anything we have the power to create. However, this is a double-edged sword because ideas are highly volatile and extremely pervasive, due to the nature of the mind, which is run by our subconscious for more than 99% of the time. We therefore absorb many ideas of which we have no conscious awareness. Yet, this is crucial to understand as these ideas literally create our experience of life.

Ideas, or thought-forms, before they become a tangible or manifested result, are fuelled by emotions. This combination of 'thoughts + emotions = feelings' is at the base of all our beliefs and values. Because of the unconscious nature of the way we absorb subconscious beliefs—which I call programmes—we find ourselves adopting and defending ideas as if they were our own, with extreme conviction, having completely forgotten—or indeed never known—where they came from. This represents the foundation that shapes our personality traits, our preferences, our choices, our potential, and therefore very much determines the kind of life we can create for ourselves.

This means that that we are hardly ever our true self, because we are acting out of subconscious beliefs 99% of the time.

The Connection Between Mind and External World

We can move a mountain with beliefs alone, or we can remain stunted and immobilized, as we keep replaying the sure evidence of how and why things are the way they are. Such is the power of our mind, and the beliefs that are repeated by it. This runs our biology, which is our state of health and energy, and predetermines how much of our potential we can access, and therefore what we can create in our life.

While some beliefs may be life enhancing, allowing our own potential to unfold, there can be a large amount that are not. These invisible thought-forms are at the root of every fear and the limitations we inadvertently carry, along with the matching feelings that are often expressed as 'It is just the way it is', or that 'Nothing can be done about it; it's in the genes!', or 'I was never very good at . . .'

Most of the influences that play a major part in our life were recorded in our first few years as an infant or a child, when we did not have conscious awareness.[5] We absorbed most of the ideas that formed our present values and beliefs before the age of 7 years old. This is illustrated in the famous quote from Aristotle: *"Give me a child until he is 7 and I will show you the man"*.

---

[5] I must add here that because of the movement of consciousness taking place, many children born in the last few years come in with exceptional self-awareness, very early on. So this comment is more relevant for people that are over 30 year old.

Between our childhood and our adult life, there has been a wide array of influences we also took on board. These are often just as reductional as the ones we registered in our first seven years, and perhaps more, due to their origin, which often comes from well-meaning people, including immediate friends and even family. Of course, this is done innocently and inadvertently, as each is subservient to their own programmed convictions. None the less, this is how hereditary blocks and limitations are passed on from generation to generation. It is a fact that, "we don't see things as they are, we see them as we are."[6]

Commercial Programming

Even now, as adults, we are constantly at the mercy of information that by-passes our conscious mind and goes straight into our subconscious mind. This shapes and influences everything we want, everything we do, and everything we think we can be. At least until we begin to 'wake up' and make use of our innate potential. In practical terms, this means that many people live someone else's dream, never realising their own, as they are too busy pursuing an illusion. While the fact that we are 'programmed' may be common knowledge today, it doesn't help in any way, unless we take responsibility and actually do something about clearing it, and regaining our human potential.

The plasticity of the subconscious mind is a well-

---

[6] Quote by Anaïs Nin

known fact that is taken advantage of by a wide array of commercial industries to get us to buy their products and services. More alarmingly, it is used to broadcast the paralysing fear-based news we absorb daily. Let's face it: news is hardly ever good! At least from the mainstream media. Fear plays a crucial role in disempowering us as it influences our mind by focusing it on 'what is wrong', so we waste valuable time 'fearing' all kinds of invisible lack. The truth is that there is plenty of everything around, including a solution for every problem. Being fearful makes it more probable that we remain controllable, gullible, so worried about 'what might go wrong' that we are far less prone to seeking how to unpack our human potential. Negative anticipation wildly practised as 'worry' pulls our focus outward, which means that we do not look within to access our most valuable source of power: the only real way out of 'fear' and 'lack'. Time to 'exit the Matrix'![7] Fear-based beliefs can fittingly be termed 'mind viruses' as they are all pervasive, constantly dominating our choices and behaviour.

The Future of Personal Science

Taking care of developing our own human potential has been disregarded for the longest time. Many still think today that it is a frivolous and somewhat useless pursuit. Yet, one day, not so far from

---

[7] Watch the film *The Matrix,* or watch again with new eyes to see past the surface.

now, personal science will be a subject featured in every school curriculum, so everyone can have access to their own potential. Right now, it has already made its way as an extra-curriculum subject in many schools and colleges, to meet the lack of fulfilment, and to address the despair and lack of wellness that so many unfortunately experience. This would be so much more relevant if personal science was treated as the essential building block that contributes to creating a successful and fulfilling life.

Introduction to NeuroBiology Reprogramming™

NeuroBiology Reprogramming™ (N.B.R.) and the part that we now come to in our journey together is about being able to clear the beliefs—the programmes—that are obstructing the natural resilience that is within you. This will naturally help you unlock more of your potential. There are many things that you once envisioned, and then gave up as 'impossible'. But right within the word 'impossible' lies 'I'm possible'. Receiving and using the next step is very much like having a 'built-in clearing system', like the anti-virus software on your computer. The computer in this case is your mind, and the clearing system, or anti-virus software, is N.B.R. This will be kept activated at its maximum functionality by your daily self-discipline.

The two steps given so far will ensure that you respond differently to what you encounter, and have the insight necessary to see what is outmoded in your own conditioning. The following step will give you the ability to literally delete it, to make room for the new.

THE ANATOMY OF THE MIND

My heartfelt intention is that the following information alleviates the self-depreciating, depressing and downright exhausting feelings, among others, that come from not understanding why the results created are so far away from one's own conscious dreams and goals. I am only able to say this because I faced the same ordeals. You have heard it said before that 'a little knowledge is a dangerous thing'. This is particularly fitting. The effect of thinking that one can create from conscious thoughts alone is squarely opposed to its original intention, which was meant to be empowering. This represents a tremendous error in thinking.

It can very simply be demonstrated by the fact that there is much we create that we did not consciously 'order'. Anyone faced with cancer—as I once was—or any other life-happenings that are less than pleasant would appreciate this. So would anyone who keeps 'failing' in business, in spite of having done 'all the right things', at least in the 20% skills area, only to be repeatedly met by failure upon failure. Although it is true that each failure brings one closer to success, lacking adequate information and the right tools often heralds being closer to giving up rather than closer to succeeding.

We cannot afford to disregard the fact many start-up businesses fail within the first few years, sometimes months, and that many newly promoted managers and leaders get demoted in the same time span.

To resolve these challenges, we have to look beyond the 20% skill part of the equation, and focus on developing the 80%, which makes up what I call our *internal wiring*. This wiring is our capacity to develop and access our own resourcefulness, which very much determines the outcomes we create in our life.

'A house divided cannot stand',[8] and least of all the mind. This is because the conscious mind is nearly always incongruent with the programmes or beliefs that are playing in the background, coming from the subconscious mind. In other words, while the conscious mind is busy designing new possibilities, the programming coming from the subconscious mind is already firmly set with a lifelong predetermined 'thermostat' that very much dictates what is possible, and what is not. The following will help you to first understand how the two parts of your mind work against each other, and then how to reconnect them so you can finally access what has eluded you.

The Mind as a Triad

The mind is made of three aspects: super-conscious, conscious and subconscious. You will see the staggering difference between the amount of

---

[8] From the Bible, *Matthew 12:25* - King James Version

information that the conscious and the subconscious mind can process. It gives a simple clue as to the chasm that exists between one's wishful thinking and the results that can be created in reality. This is very important because this also affects your physical resilience in a very real way.

Leading neuroscientist Dr. Bruce Lipton demonstrates—through studies known as epigenetics—that the hereditary factors that affect our state of health are not in fact determined by our genes, as was once thought, but are rather the product of our own subconscious programming and our environment.

"You are not 'stuck' with your genes."[9]

This is very exciting because it means that, if we have a way of clearing the programming that lies within our subconscious mind, we can literally rewrite our own history, including our state of health and energy. Said more accurately, when we simply apply the tools given here in this book, we allow Natural Intelligence to do its job, unencumbered. This is the basis of any healing.

Right here and now, we are just about to discover the easiest way of clearing these programmes, using an antidote, which is as powerful as the cause in every way: thought-forms. The following process is a marriage between science and spirituality. This is a landmark in itself, as these two disciplines have been in discord

---

[9] *The Biology of Belief*—Dr. Bruce Lipton

since the beginning of time itself. Using the following tools will not only put right personal problems, but it will also correct the limiting or destructive hereditary patterns that may still be echoing in your own life today.

But first, let us look at each part of the mind, so you can understand how this works, and satisfy our intellect, up to a point.

1. Attributes of the super-conscious mind

The super-conscious is directly and always connected with Natural Intelligence, your Inner Being and your subconscious mind. There is nothing to be done with it, other than being receptive to it, as this is the channel through which inspiration can be received and perceived. You can get inspired and receive innovative ideas simply by using your B.B.C. and B.B.M.E. steps.

2. Attributes of the subconscious mind

The subconscious mind is very accurately described by Dr. Bruce Lipton as 'a biological computer'. It is the most powerful information processor known to mankind:

- It reads our internal and external environment and works to attune our delicate biological functioning accordingly. It does so with the filter of previously recorded behaviours—the programmes—to determine a response. All of it is done with no help or knowledge from the conscious mind.

- It processes 20.000.000 environmental bits of information per second.

- It is always in the present.

- It dictates 99% of our neurobiological functioning and perceptions. It literally 'runs the show' with all mental, physical and emotional processes and responses.

- It is highly trainable—which is known in neuroscience as mind-plasticity—and replays all that was recorded into it. It will also faithfully replay any new programmes, such as new habits, practices, concepts, ideas, methods, etc.

- Along with all the great skills and neurological functioning, it also replays all recorded hurt / shock / trauma / limitations that were ever registered. A few of these are known to the conscious mind, but most of them are <u>not at all</u> and <u>can never be</u> due to its subconscious nature, and the speed and rate at which it records and processes information.

3. Attributes of the conscious mind

The conscious mind can do the five following things, but only one at a time:

1. It can make some choices, although extremely limited due to the 'perception filter' in place in the subconscious, which shapes and influences all decisions.

2. It can 'time travel' into the past and the future, or observe what is going on in the present.

3. It can make use of cognitive and intellectual faculties.

4. It can be at peace, which is its most receptive state to perceive innovative and inspired ideas.

5. It can choose to 'let go' by using the tools shared so far, or 'hang on' and remain stuck. Your increased resilience, potential and freedom hinges on this one particular function.

Having the understanding of what each part of the mind does helps to put things into perspective. As you can see, and no matter how aware anyone may be, the conscious mind remains limited and bound to the subconscious mind's predetermined programming. In fact, the conscious mind is the last part of us to register what is really going on. This is just like a great big cosmic joke. Even when thoroughly trained, and as aware as can be, the conscious mind can only realise what has already taken place. For example, if your hand came close to a candle flame, you can notice that the conscious mind hasn't much say in how far and fast you moved to avoid burning yourself. Likewise, when you are in contact with your gut feeling, that 'knowing' in your solar plexus, it is your subconscious mind that transmits what it perceives so you can have a visceral, physical experience of what it has already detected. Your physical body is directly linked to your subconscious mind. This gut feeling relays precious information, always. Very often, however, when it is perceived by the conscious mind, it is analysed, intellectualised and rationalised, only to be rejected more often than not. Yet many successful entrepreneurs listen to this precious internal compass, even if they don't know or even believe what is described in this book.

Being as consciously aware as we can is, of course, essential, and in fact primordial so we can see what is going on. However, its best and most pertinent use is to choose whether to get free or stay stuck. Such as our willpower. If we are looking to get maximum resilience, a measure of freedom, and a handle on creating seriously different results, we must do what it takes and develop the self-discipline to use what we know. Let's look closer at how our mind affects the rest of our inner and outer reality.

The Mechanism of Internal and External Creation

We have already seen the following diagram earlier in Part One. We will keep using the same diagram, and adding to it as we go through the development of resilience in each of our attributes. Right now, we are focusing on mental resilience, because it is at the origin of all other kinds of resilience.

A DIAGRAM OF YOU

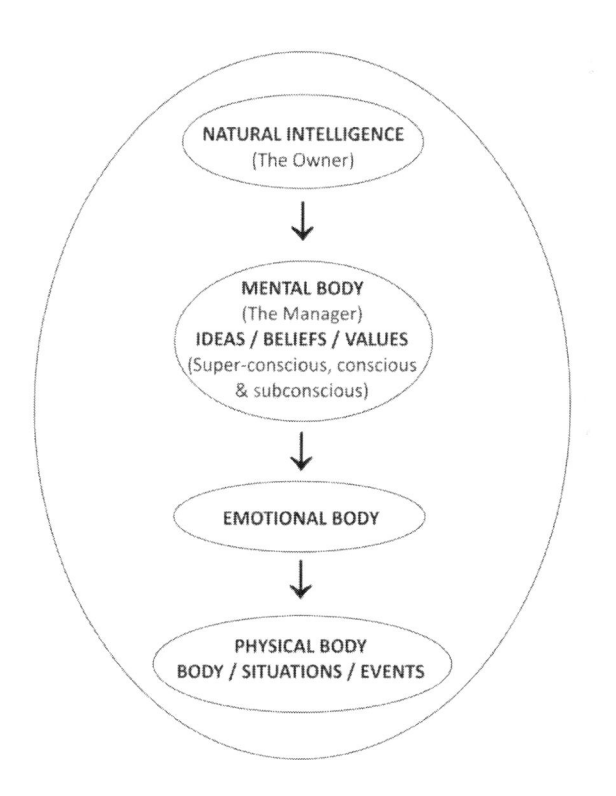

NATURAL INTELLIGENCE
(The Owner)
↓
MENTAL BODY
(The Manager)
IDEAS / BELIEFS / VALUES
(Super-conscious, conscious & subconscious)
↓
EMOTIONAL BODY
↓
PHYSICAL BODY
BODY / SITUATIONS / EVENTS

In this diagram, I call Natural Intelligence the Owner. It seems a fitting description for the awesome creative force that is the origin of our species. It also affords us to remain neutral, as many have different names for this source of power. Your preferred name is equally and absolutely fine.

Next comes the mind, here described as 'Manager'. It is important to distinguish the Manager from the Owner, because it helps us to understand and accept that there is an Intelligence greater than our own intellect. The benefit of understanding this is threefold.

First, it means that when we are limited, we can access a higher power or higher intelligence to receive help.

The second is that it helps us to understand that our mind is not who we are, but instead that with which we can see. Not unlike the headlights on a car.

Third, knowing that our intellect isn't all-ruling helps us to keep our ego in check, and prevent it from taking over. Nothing wrong with the ego, as it is part of who we are, but best to have a handle on it, lest it takes over.

The arrows signify how each part influences the next, which is why they are pointing down, from Natural Intelligence first, and then from one attribute to the other.

The mind as a whole—including conscious, subconscious and super-conscious—directly influences our emotions. Our emotions determine how we connect with ourselves and the world, through our feelings.

Thoughts + Emotions = Feeling/Beliefs

Our feelings become our beliefs, and our beliefs become our feelings.[10] There is nothing more powerful than actions derived from beliefs. This is what allows us to 'move mountains' and build all the resilience to achieve the 'impossible'. Whether these beliefs are conscious or unconscious, they dictate our attitude, our responses and what actions we take. In turn, this contributes to what we create and receive from life. This mechanism of creation is depicted by the downward arrows in the diagram.

Right now, we will reconnect the conscious and the subconscious mind, and install the clearing, or 'anti-virus', system so your conscious choices are congruent with the information that is in your subconscious.

THE PRACTICE:
NeuroBiology Reprogramming™—LEVEL ONE

I invite you to consider the following. It is both logical and based in science: The Natural Intelligence that is at our origin already orchestrates our fundamental and most intricate neurobiological

---

[10] You may have noticed by now that there is an amount of repetition in this book. This is very much a conscious choice, to help you absorb the tools and processes shared.

functions with extreme precision. Right? This source is ongoing, everlasting, and it already provides you with optimal well-being, powerful resources, unlimited potential, and natural resilience. When you look at nature itself, you can see that life force, vibrant health and abundance are everywhere. In fact, *resilience* is a mighty force that is available to anything that is organic by nature. Think about that one little plant shoot that manages to grow through concrete layers!

The resilience within you is no less amazing, for in spite of all the odds and everything that you have gone through—you are here right now, reading this, still wanting to know more, willing to review what you may be missing or learn something new . . . Wow!

Please take a breath and anchor these facts right now. If a surge of gratitude washes over you, breathe it in, and anchor it.
This is a great wiring to record in your neurobiology!

You, therefore, do not need to strive to enjoy a powerful life force, abundance, vibrant heath, or resilience, because these are your natural states—your birthrights. What is required, however, is that you clear what is obstructing this natural flow: the beliefs. Anything that disrupts, oppresses, reduces, or dilutes your potential simply needs to be cleared out. As you do, you are left with an abundance of 'raw material', otherwise known as the life force or resilience.

"What you seek is seeking you." — Rumi

Does that sound too simple?

If it does, the thought that says, 'This is far too simple, it couldn't work.', is a programme, or one of the many 'mind-viruses' we carry. The bug in the mind. It always is. It wants to solidify the beliefs that want you to stay small, unsuccessful, unfulfilled, unadventurous, doubting, depressed, or life-less.

If all is well in your life, you will find this process to be a boost wherever you choose to apply it, in your business affairs, your investments, your personal relationships, or your state of health and energy. You are limitless. Enjoy your potential.

PREPARATION FOR THE PROCESS

Reading through the following will naturally prepare you to receive the reconnection between your conscious and your subconscious mind. Don't get lost in trying to understand the first part if this isn't clear to you, reading it will do the job. Your subconscious mind will benefit. Once this is done, these two parts of your mind will begin to work with each other in a congruent manner, so one can help the other to get free from the overload of limiting beliefs. Please read it once throughout, and then once more, and then practise it.

The whole process has three parts:

1. The first is a one-time practice.

2. The second is a morning and evening daily practice, that will take about 4-6 minutes.

3. The third is the DELETE button/key: a moment per moment practice that can be used as you go about your regular activities, taking no time at all.

Part One—One-time Practice

Recognise your subconscious as the amazing entity that it is. For the first time in the history of YOU, you are going to acknowledge it. Do so as if you were greeting a long lost friend. You are. Your subconscious is a mighty entity, doing huge amounts of work. If you feel it, give it a name worthy of its awesome power and dedicated service. Depending on your learning style, you might see a name, or hear a name.

Take a quiet moment to be grateful to it. This is an amazing reunion. During seminars, many people report having had a name 'sitting at the back of their heads' their whole life. How wonderfully perceptive! If you don't have a name, please use 'Jade' if you want, until you do. This was a generic name given for everyone to use. Its use can remain permanent, or until you get your own name.

Make friends with your subconscious. It has literally been slaving away for you all our life, most of which was spent overburdened by our conscious mind repeating self-deprecating, worrying or critical thoughts. The time has come to make heartfelt amends, and to pledge not to do it again. You can simply read the italicized phrases below as often as necessary. A willingness to do what it takes and an opened heart that feels real gratitude will help to facilitate the process, and will ensure that you can feel a sense of 'coming home'. Address your subconscious mind in the following format:

Dear Jade,
Although I knew about you,
I didn't realise how much you do on a constant basis.
I simply want to say 'thank you'.

Please forgive me,
as I now realise how I have I kept you burdened by indulging in repetitive, self-deprecating thinking.

I now realise that I have kept both you and me burdened, and with it, the rest of our body and our experience of life.

In order for us to get a sense of freedom,
and to access the resilience that is already within us,
I pledge to acknowledge you every day.

The way I am going to do this is by committing to

addressing you by your name, as often as possible, and simply saying, 'I deeply appreciate everything you do', or 'I love you, and thank you'.

Please take a few full breaths, and anchor this statement with your physical gesture.

If you feel that you have established a good connection with your subconscious mind upon reading the last few lines, then it only needs to be done once.

If you feel that it needs to be repeated a few more times, do it until you feel satisfied. Begin to trust your own wisdom, which can be felt as your gut feeling or in your heart. You know best, always.

Staying out of the intellectual mind for this process is essential. Not everything can be rationalised. Just the same way that leading scientists cannot recreate the Big Bang, no matter how much expertise, time or money is being funnelled in the particle accelerator in Geneva; some things carry a 'Natural Intelligence' copyright. Some of the connectedness in this process is very much the same.

Part Two—Daily Practice

Take action: Now that you know about its awesome power, it is up to you—using your conscious mind—to win your subconscious mind's collaboration. You can do this by giving it the fuel and the energy it needs by simply practising the following breath. This breath is known as the pranayama breath.

THE PRANAYAMA BREATH
Prāṇāyāma (Sanskrit: प्राणायाम)

Pranayama is a Sanskrit word which literally means 'extension of life force'. The following breathing sequence facilitates the connection between the conscious and subconscious minds. It is very much like the conscious 'caring' for the subconscious. Breath is a nutrient for every cell, and precious information for the mind. It also provides the subconscious with the energy, the necessary fuel, required to clear limiting beliefs and blockages.

Once you have 'filled up' with this breath, the energy absorbed consciously will work throughout the day to clear limiting beliefs while your conscious mind is busy making use of its intellectual capacity. It will equally do so while the conscious mind is asleep at night. The only part of you that can 'switch off' is the conscious mind. Everything in your whole being still keeps on working.

How to prepare:

- Until you can do it amidst disturbances, make sure you disconnect all distractions so that you won't be sidetracked while you practise your breathing.

- Sit upright, with your back comfortably straight. It doesn't need to be rigidly straight.

- Put your feet flat on the ground, so you can be

'earthed' or 'grounded'.

- Let your hands rest on your lap.
- Close your eyes so you can relax deeper and count easier.
- Breathe in and out though your nose, keeping your mouth closed.

When you are ready:

- Take a breath in while mentally counting to 6.
- Hold while mentally counting to 6.
- Exhale while mentally counting to 6.
- Hold while mentally counting to 6.

This is one round; do 6 rounds.

Note: This will almost certainly take a little getting used to at first, unless you already practise some form of breathing for relaxation or yoga. This is learning a new self-discipline, so be kind to yourself in terms of keeping count, and having your mouth opened or closed. This breathing is not something you can get wrong. Allow time and patience for this training to feel easy. We all absorb new, learned habits at different rates.

Research from Harvard shows that it takes as few as 21 days, and up to 10.000 hours, to make any new practice a learned, acquired, subconscious habit. This is only an average, of course. Trust that you will find your own rhythm with this new practice. The all-important thing is to make a decision right now that you are going to do it . . . and then just do it!

The pranayama practice is best done twice a day, every day, preferably morning and night. Ideally, this is best done just before going to sleep, and before starting your day. This insures that the most important connection within you, which is between the conscious and the subconscious minds, is kept strong and nourished.

Any other form of meditation you might already be practising can be done before or after the pranayama breathing.

Part Three—The DELETE Key

Once you have read through the two parts we have just covered, you are now ready to receive your clearing tool. This tool will literally erase limitations the moment you become aware of them, and use it. Because you will have developed internal and external awareness by practising your B.B.C. and B.B.M.E., it will be easier for you to notice them.

You may recognise limitations through your feelings, your self-talk and through your involvement with others, in the words you speak, and the decisions and actions you take.

To ensure that you can literally erase a limiting belief as it arises, the tool that you are getting is in every way as fast and as powerful as the element that is creating the blockage: a thought-form. This thought-form is called the DELETE key. Its effect is very similar to the delete key you use on your computer.

Delete

The two main differences with this DELETE key is that it is a virtual tool, something you just say mentally, and it will literally act like an anti-virus software in your subconscious mind. Using it is what will clear your subconscious mind of its programming. Don't worry, this will not erase any of the useful skills you have!

In order to make this thought-form highly useable, I am going to suggest that you select a colour for your DELETE key. If you are doubting the effect that such a virtual tool can have on the mind, rest assured and know that it is in every way as good as the virtual technology you use on a daily basis; for example, when you send texts and emails. You will be able to DELETE the beliefs that you want to clear as easily as deleting the emails you don't want. It will not cost any great emotional loss or concern, quite the contrary. Let's just say that you are accessing some of your quantum computing capacities. The DELETE key will make the process of clearing limiting beliefs the fastest and most efficient. It allows you to clear limiting thoughts as they arise, without needing to wait until a later time, which probably means it would never get done, or add to your to-do list, which is probably long enough as it is.

Right now, please pick a colour that appeals to you. Take a moment to do this as you read these words. There is not time like the present! Once you have it, associate it to the delete button included on the last page. If choosing the colour is causing you to be bothered in any way, forget it! Keep it as you see it on the page, black and white. The colour is not necessary. It is only useful if you find it useful.

Note: If your learning style is *kinaesthetic*, you might literally like to draw this out and fill it in with your chosen colour. It will 'imprint' better on both your conscious and your subconscious minds.

If your learning style is *visual*, simply visualise this delete button in your chosen colour, or in black and white if you prefer.

If your learning style is *auditory*, simply say DELETE verbally if you are on your own, or mentally if there are people around you.

Once this has become a habit, some practitioners find the colour handy as its association with other things of the same colour remind them of their DELETE key. Let's face it, there is often a belief that is best if cleared out, and the easier it is to do, the better.

How to Use the DELETE Key

Anytime you perceive judgement or blame, toward yourself, another or a situation, see or mentally say DELETE. Using this DELETE key on the perceived judgement is the mechanism of *letting go*.

When you use it, the particular belief that caused you to be limited, worried or fearful will be cleared, meaning that it will no longer elicit the usual emotional response. This means that this belief, which is really just a memory, will be 'disabled'. While the memory itself may still resurface, you will not be subservient to it, as a thought without any emotional attachment has little to no power. In fact, seeing a memory without suffering the emotions attached to it can give you the discernment necessary to not make the same mistake twice.

Once there is room or space in your mind, it means that you are receptive and can hear, see or perceive the solution, if one is required.

If you are not in need of any solution, clearing mind-clutter can allow you to have complete peace of mind. This in itself can seriously boost your resilience level.

Alternatively, and for those of you who feel the need to 'understand' how this works, you can also use the phrase 'I release you from . . .' whenever you perceive a limiting belief, critical thoughts toward self or others, or feelings or worry and fear of lack. You are speaking from your conscious mind, addressing your subconscious mind. As a reminder, only the conscious mind has the power of letting go of a belief. The subconscious mind faithfully runs the programmes that were recorded into it. It cannot free itself unless the conscious mind chooses to let go.

Example: Using lack of self-confidence as an example, you can think or mentally say the following phrase 'Jade, I release you from self-doubt.' Or you can simply apply the DELETE key when you are entertaining thoughts of self-disapproval, self-criticism, etc.

Using Your Physical Anchor

Once you are familiar with the process, please use the same physical anchor you chose in Part One of this book, following the B.B.C. and the B.B.M.E. practices. Just like for these practices, using your physical anchor to record this new routine will help it to be more permanent, as you are literally teaching your body-mind—your neurobiology—a new response. This is what makes this practice more solid, more tangible and more accessible in the moment you need it.

Please also take a conscious breath when you use this clearing process. Circulating this new state of freedom throughout your whole body is very beneficial. Even if all you get is a tiny amount of relief, for a fraction of a second, it is still worth anchoring. Please see the examples following and the Q&A session coming up.

WHEN AND WHY TO USE NEUROBIOLOGY REPROGRAMMING™

When?

Use the full NeuroBiology Reprogramming™ process whenever you note that one of your particular values or beliefs no longer serves you, or is in the way to creating something you want. You can also use it when you feel unwell, whether emotionally, physically or mentally, or if you are feeling too much fear or worry.

You can also use NeuroBiology Reprogramming™ when you are thriving, when you feel great and happy, and would like to access more of your potential. Perhaps you would like to take an area of your life to the next level. This would be a great idea because there is much more potential available to you that you haven't yet unpacked.

You can use N.B.R. whether you want to clear something that you perceive is in you, or another. How does that work? Because we do not see people or situations as they really are, but rather as we are.

This is very much like wearing a pair of glasses, with our own perception smeared over the lenses.

So, no matter what we notice, if we are willing to take responsibility, everyone wins. This will do much to transform the quality of your relationships, and the way you interact with the world at large. There is always a myriad of other perceptions that could be gleaned by interacting with another, but the interaction is limited to your particular experience of life so far, and your perceptions. Even if these are very broad, it still takes a massive, conscious effort to broaden one's mind and allow who or what we are encountering to be perceived more fully. Think of it as the difference between a child looking at a tree leaf, touching it, tasting it, examining it, actually experiencing it, and an adult just saying, 'Ah yes! There's an oak leaf!' In the case of the adult, there is an immediate 'mental tagging' of the leaf, which doesn't leave any chance for the leaf to be experienced. In the case of the child, there is the discovery of the leaf, for the sake of the experience itself.

You can also use NeuroBiology Reprogramming™ when you don't know what you consciously want to change: there is plenty in us that holds us up, that we do not perceive since it is in subconscious form. Sometimes we just feel blocked. In this case, we can simply say, 'Jade, I release you from feeling 'blocked'.' without needing to understand exactly where the blockage is coming from. The Natural Intelligence that is already orchestrating your full human mechanism knows where to allocate your 'letting go' decision.

As I mentioned previously, not every piece of this process can be intellectualised. Far from it. Often, and when it comes to tapping into your awesome and vast human potential, you have to develop 'faith' or 'trust' in the power that is already beating your heart, or giving you your next breath. I can't imagine why anyone would not have impeccable trust in it, as it is doing a pretty good job by all accounts.

When a belief has already gone through the whole manifestation process, as depicted by the downward arrows in the diagram, it can take longer to shift. You may find yourself using your DELETE key for the same belief for some time. This is a process that you can use daily for as long as is required. To help yourself, and to make sure you shift it, I would recommend that you take a new decision and make a new step in the direction of what you want to change or experience. There are exercises coming up that will help you do that.

For most people, using this process will mean that it is the first time that their mind is connected, and that they feel 'at one' with themselves. They are enjoying a renewed sense of fulfilment, not tied to an external event or a person, and not attached to any outcomes. The best and most real kind of fulfilment.

This is also the first time that the conscious and the subconscious minds work as one, which makes achieving goals or manifesting your heart's desire a lot easier. This is because both minds are moving in the same direction, rather than working against each other. They are now congruent with one another.

7 Good 'Whys' to Practice N.B.R.

1. While you may not have any control in a particular situation, you always have the choice to react as you will, and to attribute a particular meaning to it. So if you choose to use any situation as an occasion to practise, you will acquire a level of awareness and wisdom that can equal 20-30 years of self-discipline. This is because each time that one more person joins in the collective consciousness, and contributes to it by their daily practise, the field of consciousness literally increases, and becomes a little more steady, and a little more real. This means that it becomes more readily accessible to everyone, even if they haven't done this sort of work before.

    Think back 10-20 years and see how many organisations might have required services such as personal development programmes teaching mindfulness and resilience. Not many, I think you will agree. Now look at what is going on today. There are fewer businesses, no matter the size, that do not provide some kind of personal development or wellness programmes for their employees. This can benefit individuals, and in turn contribute to improving the culture, which undoubtedly affects sales and customer satisfaction.

2. Even if, for some reason, you choose not to practise the steps given upon finishing this book, knowing

that you have the choice to do so is empowering in itself. It means that if you remain stuck, you now have the proof that it is due to a choice you are making, and not someone else's fault. This actually puts you in the driver's seat.

3. Being able to take responsibility for our own perceptions can be a tremendous contribution in conflict prevention or conflict resolution. It allows us to become 100% responsible for how we contribute to any event, which can literally create different scenarios. It can even put an end to a recurrent type of event we may be experiencing, that we want to eliminate from our lives.

    Equally empowering is the fact that greater foresight, and the ability to delete our own pre-determined mindset can enable us to anticipate problems and challenges ahead of time. This can give us the advantage of seeking, and therefore receiving, a timely solution.

4. Each time you are willing to release thoughts and beliefs that limit your well-being and restrict your potential, you can become more closely who you are at the core. It means that the same Natural Intelligence that created you can 'get a hand in' restoring your natural health, energy and enthusiasm. The less burdened you are with limited beliefs, the more internal space you have, and because nature hates a void, it will be filled with

what you need most at that particular time.

5. For many people, the beliefs that are creating the limitations come from a lack of self-worth, and self-esteem. The benefits derived from this clearing practice will then be a renewed sense of self-appreciation, or forgiveness or even compassion, if self-love is not readily accessible.

   Clearing up such a hold is important because a lack of self-worth can be very far reaching, affecting personal relationships as well as professional endeavours. So having the right tools makes it easier to shift through old blockages and take bold steps forward.

6. Each thought we entertain fires neurotransmitters into motion. This produces particular molecules that we perceive as emotions, right before this becomes a physical state. For example, feeling peace or gratitude means that 'happy hormones' are being produced in our body. It also means that our internal physiological environment is alkaline, which is the base for vibrant health and regeneration. Because our intricate biological environment works in a close community, we are more likely to receive inspired ideas when we are at peace. We also have more physical energy to make steady progress, which makes it far more likely that we can create the success intended.

   Worry, stress or hatred, on the other hand,

create an acidic environment in the body. An acidic environment is the root cause of most illnesses. It is very difficult to see and to grab opportunities when we feel worried, stressed, because whatever flows through our mind literally shapes our brain. We often end up making all the wrong moves.

7. NeuroBiology Reprogramming™ demands your complete willingness to take full responsibility for what is going on in you and in your life. Please take note that I am not saying that things are your fault. What I am saying is that the only way you can turn things around is by taking responsibility for your own mindset, as this is at the origin of your whole experience. No one else can do that for you. No one else can free you but yourself.

As you recognise your manifested world as your teacher, your cue to practise self-discipline, you will undoubtedly begin to feel a measure of freedom, gratitude and ultimate resilience.

Look at it this way: unless a particular problem came up, you wouldn't have had a chance to clear the beliefs attached to it. If you didn't get a chance at clearing it, the same reality would keep on replaying, until you take note. This is largely why anything happens repeatedly. This may be an area that you really want to excel in or transform, so unless you get to clear the 'wall' that stands between you and it, it is very unlikely that you will get the results you want. This means that you end up being grateful for a limit to come up, as it gives you the opportunity to access what is right behind it. This is the ultimate resourcefulness, the ultimate resilience.

There are literally hundreds and thousands of programmes that run 'at the back' of our mind, in our subconscious. Below are some examples of how to use N.B.R., and following this are a few lists of common limiting beliefs gathered over the years from doing clearing on people.[11]

Examples

Example 1—Imagine that you said: 'My boss is a tyrant!'

How do you feel when you declare this? Probably disempowered and victimized, or angry, closed down and maybe even revengeful. I think you will agree that none of these feelings are conducive to bettering the situation, or your feelings about it. You might say to me, 'But I am absolutely right! He really is a tyrant!' which, of course, may be partly true. This is how to apply what we have learnt so far . . .

---

[11] A full online programme to clear beliefs is available at www.drdugast.com

'My boss is a tyrant!'

Address your subconscious with the name you chose, or use 'Jade'.

- Think, say or see the DELETE button (in your own colour) to release the belief, judgement and blame.
- When you feel a little mental-emotional relief, take a regular breath to circulate this state throughout your whole body, and use your physical gesture to anchor it.

OR

o You can mentally say, 'Jade, I release you from 'judgement'.'
o When you feel a little mental-emotional relief, take a regular breath to circulate this state throughout your whole body, and use your physical gesture to anchor it.

If you practise this enough, it will completely change your perception. If you are also linking your clearing with your physical gesture, you might even find your hand doing the motion you selected, before you are consciously aware and choosing to use your clearing tool. This is when things get really easy.

When you are willing to let go of your own beliefs, you can begin to feel the peace that is already within you. When there is peace in you, you see things in a different light, and new possibilities are available for all. When just one person—you—is willing to take responsibility to 'let go', it creates the space for something new to happen. Nothing new can happen while you hold on to a particular belief, as this is very much the cement that holds a particular situation in place. If you could see the energy between people, you would see how they are like cords between people, and that even if one person is willing to disengage their involvement, it can change the dynamics of the interaction. This is more science than anything else.

For you, this actually means that you will be guided or inspired to take different actions, which will create different results.

For anyone else: it's not our business!

Example 2—'My partner is not very loving.'

The chances are, if you have declared this, your feelings and actions match your words. You are also grappling with your own closure mechanism, whatever that looks like for you.[12] You are probably not feeling loved back, not making any efforts, feeling sad, alone, unloved, and unseen. Perhaps even unworthy. As you now know, these beliefs are replaying from your own subconscious mind. They are made 'visible' through an external situation—in the situation you are describing—so you can have a chance to clear them. It is very simple. When you do, a different dynamic can enter the relationship, starting with you doing something

---

[12] See *Healing the Divide Between Man & Woman*, a free eBook available at www.drdugast.com

different.

'My partner is not very loving'

Address your subconscious with the name you chose, or use 'Jade'.

- Think, say or see the DELETE key (in our own colour) to release this belief, which is based in judgement and blame.

- When you feel a little mental-emotional relief, take a regular breath to circulate this state throughout your whole body, and use your physical gesture to anchor it.

OR

o Mentally say, 'Jade, I release you from 'judgement' and 'blame'.'

o When you get a little relief, take a regular breath to circulate this state throughout your whole body, and use your physical gesture to anchor it.

Note: Regarding personal relationships, we can only receive the love we think we deserve, which is the love we really have for ourselves. So it is always best to look at one's own relationship to self, first and always. The beautiful thing is that with this practice—the full N.B.R. method—you will actually begin to fully appreciate who you are. A large part of the internal split anyone feels actually comes from the fragmentation between the conscious and the subconscious minds. This is why people don't like some part of them. The funny thing is that these parts are actually only beliefs, and until they are cleared out, both your conscious and subconscious minds suffer. Along with the rest of you.

As you simply read through the reconnecting exercise earlier on, which you can do every day or until you feel that it is 'done', an amount of healing already took place in you. You will not be the same person by the time you finish reading this book, as even just reading about it allows you to be 'reconnected' with yourself. This work is really non-retractable, which means that once you are aware of it, you cannot really pretend you don't know. This will change the nature of your relationship with yourself, and with others around you as a consequence.

As mentioned earlier, expectations are killers, especially in relationships. When we expect, we are waiting for the effort to come from anyone else but ourselves. Instead, we can be willing to communicate truly, which is the base for intimacy, and be as present as can be by tuning in to our B.B.C. step. Being able to share a vulnerability with our beloved means that we are taking responsibility rather than using blame or judgement. It creates a very different outcome.

A good question, worth asking, once you have done your clearing could be 'What can I do for you, so that you feel absolutely loved?' I can guarantee you a transformation of the relationship with these few simple tools.

Example 3—'I am not worthy of financial abundance' or 'Money is the root of all evil'

Address your subconscious with the name you chose, or use 'Jade'.

- Think, say or see the DELETE key (in your own colour) to release this belief, which is based in lack and fear (often rooted in religion, or something heard during childhood).
- When you feel a little mental-emotional relief, take a regular breath to circulate this state throughout your whole body, and use your physical gesture to anchor it.

OR

o Mentally say, 'Jade, I release you from 'lack' and 'fear'.'
o When you feel a little mental-emotional relief, take a regular breath to circulate this state throughout our whole body, and use your physical gesture to anchor it.

We literally hold hundreds of beliefs, some consciously, and many more subconsciously. These are in the way of receiving what we really want, or of finding a solution to a recurrent problem.

In the next chapter, there is an exercise that will help you to first identify what area you would like to work on, and a series of self-inquires so you can apply and make it work for you right now.

The following is a sample of some common beliefs that are in the way of resilience, in some popular topics.

Sample List of Limiting Beliefs

Business / money / career:
1. This company doesn't pay very well.
2. My employees are lazy and ungrateful.
3. I was never good with money.
4. Pursuing what I love will not make me an income.
5. This is not a good time to start a business; I am more likely to fail right now.
6. Investing is risky.
7. I spend money like there is no tomorrow.
8. Rich people are cruel, mean, evil, drug dealers.
9. I am too old to start investing / to create a business I love.
10. There is too much competition out there.

Health / energy:
1. I have done everything I can to lose weight.
2. Tomorrow, I will . . .
3. Life isn't worth living without chips, chocolate and soda.
4. I need alcohol to celebrate.
5. I have less energy because that is just the way it

is when you get older.
6. This . . . (particular problem) cannot be transformed because it runs in the family.
7. I didn't inherit the good genes.
8. There is no point, I am 'big boned'.
9. I don't have what it takes.
10. You can't have your cake and eat it.

Relationships / love:
1. All the good men or women are taken.
2. My kids are don't have any respect for me.
3. True love and passion cannot last.
4. He doesn't see me / understand me.
5. She doesn't appreciate me.
6. Loving myself would mean that I am vain.
7. Marriage is a story of convenience.
8. If he or she . . . (did something to help the relationship), or behaved like . . . we might have a chance to make this work.
9. A relationship should flourish on its own.
10. All men or women are liars, and I don't want to get hurt again.

Most beliefs we entertain are 'family programs', meaning that have been passed on for generations, by simply being repeated enough times. Some beliefs are developed due to a repeated lack of self-worth, which is also the result of recurrent internal conversations with ourselves. The good news is that all of them can be cleared, using your DELETE key. Remember when there is peace in you, there is space. When there is space in you, the creator in you—Natural Intelligence—can inspire you to feel differently, and act differently as you take different steps, which will certainly create different results.

Q&A

Q: Is the breathing given here the same as in the B.B.C. practice?

A: No. The breathing talked about in tuning in to your B.B.C. is simply about observing your regular, natural breathing mechanism. Focusing on it a few minutes allows you to get a break from your mind-emotion reaction, and allows you to reconnect with your core self, or Inner Being, where all is always well.

The pranayama breathing is a breathing technique that allows your conscious and subconscious to communicate. In particular because the subconscious cannot free itself from any beliefs, only the conscious mind can decide to do that. Your subconscious mind has already been unacknowledged your whole life, so the pranayama breathing insures that some energy goes to it. Breath is love, information, energy, and acknowledgement. This will insure that your subconscious has the necessary energy to process a clearing you might decide on before you go to sleep, or at the beginning of your day, while your conscious mind is asleep, or forgets during the day.

Q: Why is it important to practise this particular breathing, and could I get away with not doing it?

A: Self-discipline is a key to success, and, in this case, it includes a breathing that will take you no more than 3 minutes, twice a day. The investment is worth it in every way, as it will yield many dividends.

The thing you might like to do is ask yourself why you are considering 'getting away with not doing it'? The answer to this question will reveal one of your programmes. It could be a significant one, which, from experience, probably stands right before many things you wish you had the energy to achieve. DELETE it, and you will be able to change your life.

Here are some more ways that you can benefit from practicing the pranayama breathing:

1. On a most fundamental and basic level, and because of our daily busy-ness, we don't breathe in deep enough to recycle the air throughout the whole lungs, which means that there always remains an amount of stale air inside our lungs. Limited oxygen means limited potential for each of our 50 trillion cells. Practising the pranayama breathing literally retrains the body to breathe deeper, slower, and naturally increase your own natural regenerating and rejuvenating capacity. Peace feels good, and looks good on everyone!

2. Breath is energy, information and potential for our cells and our whole Being, which includes mental, emotional, spiritual, and physical layers. You can consider breath as a source of indispensable energy—also known as 'mana' or 'chi'—which is as important as water is to a plant. Because we run around all day, most of the time breathing very shallowly, it means that we are depleted from our most vital and important nutrient. Practising this simple breathing means that our energy bank account is always full.

3. Practising the pranayama breath is a way to acknowledge and take care of your Inner Being, and your subconscious mind. You can consider this exercise an act of care and love, to restore the internal relationship between the conscious and the subconscious minds. It very much is. This is a delicate relationship, that has been fragmented since the beginning of your existence so every care needs to be taken to make sure this becomes a working relationship. In fact, and because this is just like any other you may be involved in, you will find that the quality of your relationships is in direct proportion with your own, internal relationship. Remember that the processing capacity of the subconscious mind and its overriding role accounts for more than 95% of your state of health and

energy,[13] your potential and your experience of life.

Over the years, and having delivered this work in many different countries, I have seen time and again that the lack of self-love, self-confidence, or the feeling that we are 'not [something] enough' comes from this internal mental fragmentation. There are many subconscious beliefs that are the root cause of self-disapproval. The symptoms include a wide range of mechanisms, aimed at attempting to 'fill the gap', to make up for the sense of lack being experienced. Filling the gap can be, in its mildest form, acquiring new possessions or seeking new experiences, hoping that this will fill the void being experienced. In the worst case scenario, this gap is filled by addictions of all kinds: meaningless sex, gambling, drugs, alcohol, food, shopping, etc. Using this breathing daily is the beginning of re-establishing self-care. It can be done in bed and is a wonderful way to begin and end the day.

4. While you sleep, your conscious mind is inactive, but your subconscious keeps on working, 24/7. If you decide to release a particular belief or problem, and have done your breathing regularly so there is a good connection between your conscious and subconscious minds, your subconscious mind will be

---

[13] See page 137 of *The Biology of Belief* by Dr. Bruce Lipton for two illustrated depictions of the subconscious mind. Seeing can help.

able to process the clearing while you sleep. All you need to do is to name what you want to transform before you go to sleep. This breathing practice means that there is sufficient energy, or mana, in you, so that what you want to release can be processed. I don't know of any other processes that can work for you in this way on the planet. You have the simplest, most powerful, fastest, most unobtrusive and effective tool at your disposal. All you have to do is breathe.

5. The breath is the first nutrient for the body, and source of potential. With practise, and as you become unencumbered by former mindset limitations, you will be able to literally 'breathe in' any solution you need. It looks like this: if you DELETE the belief that you cannot achieve something as you exhale a breath, it is a possibility that the solution, which is contained in your next inhalation, will be configured by your mind. While this simple process can literally happen with every breath, it will be made more possible if your daily self-discipline incudes this breathing practice. It doesn't take much longer than brushing your teeth, just twice daily.

I have 'breathed in' solutions countless times, when I get stuck with some new IT, for example. My belief would have been 'I don't know how to use it', and once I release this from my mind, somehow, I can always find the solution. It works.

Q: If I use the delete button to a particular thought or belief, does that mean it won't ever come back?

A: This is a new habit, so it is the same as with any new practice. Just like you would not reasonably expect to have final results from going to the gym just once or a few times, you might need to delete the same belief several times until it no longer has an emotional charge attached to it. Beyond clearing any belief, using your own resilience by actually taking a step in the direction of what you want to experience will help tremendously, and determine how fast it goes. Ultimately, and if you are ready for a breakthrough, the clearing takes effect in the moment that it is done. An idea without the emotional charge is just an idea. It is harmless. While an idea may resurface, it will not affect you once the clearing has been done.

Something to bear in mind, however, is that it is best to surrender once you have cleared an old belief. Programmes such as control, doubt and lack of trust are all rooted in fear, and are best cleared if and when they arise. Fear-based beliefs have a lot of momentum, as they are unfortunately prevalent all around us. Choose carefully who you talk to, as each is tied to their own programming. In fact, seeking external reassurance may be in the way of your getting free from a particular belief, because while you can expect anything from yourself, you cannot control people's reactions, especially if they are used to you in a particular context. Instead, you could choose to talk to people that challenge you to grow and force you to stretch outside your comfort zone. A good coach is an excellent choice.

It often happens that the most dramatic results are seen in hindsight. This is great because it means that you took your focus off 'expecting results', and instead focused on taking new steps to help yourself, and make your success more certain.

Q: How long does the breathing take?

A: About 3 minutes in the morning and the same at night.

Q: Can it be added to other practices?

A: Sure. If you practise other things, such as meditation, or any other disciplines, this breathing can be practised before or after, or anytime that suits you.

Q: How can I practise saying, seeing or mentally saying 'Jade, I release you from . . .' while I listen to someone talk and be present to them?

A: You may not realise it, but as you interact with anyone, there is a constant 'mental conversation' taking place. The mind is busy emitting judgement, comparison, etc. So instead of letting the mind run riot—as it does when it is untrained—you are choosing to harness its power. As you pay attention and notice what is going on within your own mind, you can simply choose to clear limiting beliefs, judgement or comparison when they arise. The space created in you is often experienced in yourself and equally felt by others as 'presence'. There is nothing better than interacting with someone who is fully present, in personal or professional dealings.

Using your DELETE key while you interact with others can help you to free yourself from many of your own beliefs. This is because the things that resonate with you and affect you most deeply only do so because you have an emotional connection to them. As you listen deeply, in a state of presence, clearing what comes up in you, everyone can receive what they need. The person talking to you feels heard and you speak clearer, which means you can also be inspired with words that may not have come through you otherwise. We will explore more about communication and listening skills in Chapter 9.

Q: Why can't I simply use positive affirmations?

A: Willpower is a tremendous force, but it only harnesses the power of the conscious mind. While it is of course possible to make fundamental changes with one decision only, the resilience required to see a new decision to completion may be affected by underlying subconscious beliefs. This may not appear clearly until the same problem is re-enacted. This can show up in the form of a different situation, yet producing the same outcome, the same problem or limitation. For example, 'different partner, same problem' or 'new business but same failed attempt at success'.

Did you ever take a decision on the 1st of January and drop it within days? The phrase 'we are creatures of habit' is rooted in the fact that we are subservient to our own subconscious programmes. If you are old enough to have used tapes (from tape recorders) you will know that recording a new piece of music over an old piece doesn't quite work out. At some point, the old piece of music resurfaces and can be heard in the background, ruining the present symphony. Similarly, some of our patterns are deeply engrained and can be challenging to shift. A conscious decision is often not enough to shift it fully.

Example: Let's say that you are now in a new relationship, and have consciously decided not to react in a particular way when your partner says or does something that usually triggers you. Let's say that this is the same problem that ended every other relationship prior to this new one. You will find that making a conscious decision to react otherwise is certainly the beginning of being able to shift an old habit, but you may also find that permanently shifting a habitual and automatic—subconscious—programmed response is a 'mammoth' task. You might find that, in the moment you got triggered, your mouth said things before you could catch any of the words.

The way you will know that your own programming has been erased is when you no longer get triggered when you are met by the same type of remark or attitude. Better still, with enough clearing, your 'emitting signal' will have shifted enough for you to attract a different kind of partner. This is valid, as always, for personal and professional relationships.

However, once you clear what is in the way, you will find that positive affirmations can reach further and faster, and produce better results. In fact, I will give you a last practice so you can make maximum use of your mind in Chapter 10, in The Master Plan. This will insure that you can create fast and unprecedented results.

Q: How can I know if what I am thinking is inspired or programmed?

A: This is a great question. Let me give you two simple markers you can apply anywhere, anytime. A fantastic habit to develop is self-inquiry. It will give you the wisdom of seeing consequences before you take action. So when you hear an idea, or feel 'pulled' to doing something, simply ask yourself:

1. Does the thought I am entertaining or the decision I am about to make benefit others in some way, or just myself?

2. Upon the application of that same decision, or actualising that thought, will I effectively be leaving a profit or a deficit behind me?

This self-inquiry can be adapted to financial, structural (within an organisation), physical, emotional, or in any other way that you are querying one of your insights. If you find that the answer is 'no' to one or both of these self-inquiries, I suggest that you would review the decision you are considering. Simply keep using your NeuroBiology Programming™ steps until the idea you are thinking can produce more positive than negative outcomes. Please don't think that there are 'rules' across the board for the various ideas anyone may entertain. You have to look at your own life, where you have come from, and what you want to create to determine the best answer. Your own history is at stake, as every thought and every action falls under the law of cause and effect. In general, leaving a profit behind you will ensure that more of the same comes your way.

When 'no' is the answer to either or both of these queries, it means that the present idea may be coming from programmed thinking, or that you may be acting out of fear. This usually produces limited results, if any.

Not all programmed thinking is bad, however, as one may choose to duplicate an idea in their own company that they heard somewhere else. You can apply the same self-inquiry to make sure this will work in your particular business. I would, however, still allow inspired thinking, as this is precisely what can make 'a very good' idea an 'absolutely outstanding' one.

Q: Is having a lot of positive beliefs a good thing, or must you clear them too?

A: It all depends on how you use them. If they give you the emotional fuel to be well and create the results you have in mind: all well and good. If, however, they also become your standards for people around you, and if your well-being, productivity or happiness relies on everyone adopting them, you are going to suffer. This means that you have gone into expectations. In this case, 'expectations' would be the belief to release.

Example: If your good mood at home depends on your spouse being happy, even if he or she doesn't feel it, it means that you won't be satisfied. Instead, you can take care of yourself, and your own positivity to radiate through your actions, your words and your gestures. As you know by now, you create your situation from the inside out, not the outside in. I often have one spouse taking the online course, and the other seeing such a change in their partner that they too want to take the course. This is much better than expecting someone else to change. This is taking great responsibility.

The bottom line is that we affect the world by simply looking at it, even before we say or do anything, as we emit powerful electromagnetic frequencies. While this may be hard to believe, it is actually the basis of quantum physics. If 'seeing' helps you to believe, although you need to believe to be able to see, have a look on YouTube at the Double Slit experiment.[14] This is what allowed us to accept that we influence what we come into contact with and begin the journey and exploration of quantum physics.

Ultimately, you don't want to rely on anyone for your happiness or your success. Whatever you seek must be an internal state before it can become a steady, tangible experience. If you rely on people and external situations for your well-being, your success or your happiness, you will always be at their mercy, and your feeling will remain conditional. This would not be true freedom or true resilience.

If you don't go 'within', you go 'without'!

Q: Is there anything that I dislike around me, at work or in my partner, that has nothing whatsoever to do with my own programming?

A: Events in your life, people you are associated with, and any situation you are involved in helps you to see your own beliefs, both conscious and subconscious. It is quite like being at the theatre, except that the scenes you are watching and the characters acting in it reflect your own values and beliefs externally, so you can see clearer what is really going on inside you. You can accurately say that your direct reality gives you a chance

---

[14] See Thomas Young's finding 'The Double Slit experiment' 1801 – available on YouTube.

to see what you have been thinking, and what you have been feeling, so you can change your mindset and create a different outcome.

While it may demand that you grow beyond what you are observing, know that this is always within your power and potential. It wouldn't be happening if it were not. Such is your power.

LET'S TALK STORY!

An Ancient Zen Story, Adapted to Modern Times

A Zen master was visiting New York City. He came upon a hot dog stand and decided to try the famous American street food.

'What would you like with your hot dog?' offered the vendor.

'Make me one with everything, please!' said the Zen master.

The vendor prepared a hot dog and handed it to the Zen master, who handed over a $50 note in exchange.

The vendor put the note in his cash box and closed it.

The Zen master waited a few seconds, and seeing that there was no sign of any change coming back, he asked, 'Excuse me, but where is my change?'

To which the hot dog vendor responded, 'Change must come from within.'

CHAPTER 5—PRACTICE RECAP

N.B.R. LEVEL I: MENTAL RESILIENCE

THE PRACTICE: NeuroBiology Reprogramming™

Part One: One-time practice
- Name your subconscious and read through the reconnecting statement.

Part Two: Daily practice
- Pranayama breathing morning and night.

Part Three: Clearing tools
- Apply your DELETE key (in your own colour) or mentally say, 'I release you from . . .' to clear any limiting beliefs.
- Take a regular breath to circulate this clearing around your whole body, and use your physical gesture to anchor it.

The B.B.C., B.B.M.E. and the step above is the full NeuroBiology Reprogramming™.

CHAPTER 6

TAKING NEUROBIOLOGY REPROGRAMMING™ ON THE ROAD

"It's easy to figure out the nature of your subconscious programs. Just take a look at the character of your life. It's a printout of your subconscious programs."

— Dr. Bruce Lipton

Now that you are fully equipped to clear out what does not serve you, let's make use of it and see what areas you want to improve upon, or take to the next level. If you are unsure as to where to begin, the results from the following exercise will help you prioritise.

EXERCISE—PART 1
How Smooth Is Your Ride?

The Wheel Of Life Self-Inquiry

Take a moment to look at the areas included in your Wheel of Life. You can either write directly in the book if you are reading a paper version, or simply make notes aside if you are reading the electronic format.[15]

The circle in the centre represents zero, and the number 10, in the small circle, is at the edge of the wheel. Fill in the rest of the numbers by grading each line from 0 to 10. The number 10 signifies contentment and fulfilment in that particular area, and 0 would indicate that you are experiencing a lack of fulfilment or struggles on that area. An example follows shortly with a case study of someone I will call Trevor to protect confidentiality.

---

[15] This whole course is available as an online practitioner and teacher training. It can also be taken without certification. Visit www.drdugast.com

THE WHEEL OF YOUR LIFE

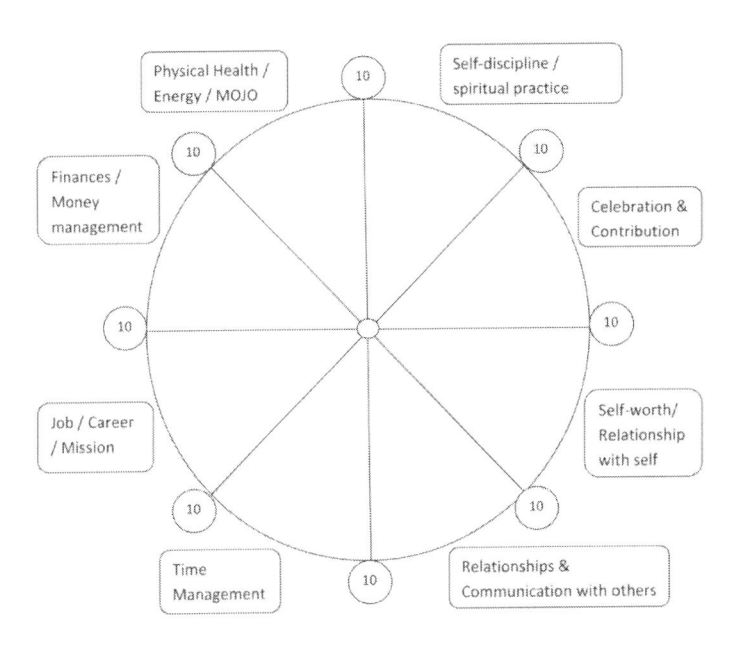

Wheel diagram with eight segments labeled: Physical Health / Energy / MOJO, Self-discipline / spiritual practice, Celebration & Contribution, Self-worth / Relationship with self, Relationships & Communication with others, Time Management, Job / Career / Mission, Finances / Money management. Each segment marked with 10.

When this is done, you are ready for a self-assessment. Take a moment to evaluate each area in the wheel as it applies to you as of today, with zero being the lowest score, where you feel really dissatisfied, and 10 being where you feel completely satisfied.

Is Your Ride Smooth or Bumpy?

Let me reassure you and say that 'bumpy' is quite normal. The only thing that matters is that you become aware of what needs your attention, and use your tools to improve it, take it to the next level, and perhaps even to clear a belief before it provides a hard jolt or a 'reality check'. In any case, this wheel can give you the necessary foresight in readiness for changes.

If you find that one particular area is already showing results that you are not at all happy with, don't worry. Instead, know that you have the exact tools to be able to turn anything around, as nothing is set in stone. Remember that anything that is actualised began as a thought-form, and then became an emotion. So things can change the moment you think different thoughts.

Now that you can clearly see what is going on for you, you can ask yourself:

1. Are you surprised by your findings, or were you already aware of what needed your attention?

2. Even though there may be several you would like to work on, for now, which element do you feel is most relevant to increasing your resilience level?

3. Are you truly ready to do what it takes to make the changes necessary?

4. Why do you want to gain resilience or improve in that particular area? It is very important that you find the answer to this question, as this will give you the energy required to initiate the change, and the staying power to see it through to completion.

Note: This is an evaluation you can do periodically, about every three months, for example. You will see that this wheel will change and evolve as you do, and according to the level of awareness and the energy you have at any given point.

This is also because one belief may be the 'entry-point' to many more. This is normal, as we hold hundreds and thousands of beliefs. Let me reassure you and say that the whole clearing process gets easier as you use it. Deleting any thought-form will eventually not take any more energy than blinking an eye. Until it is a learned habit, however, you have to put in the practice time.

As you set off to make changes in your preferred area, please begin with a 'bite size' piece you can handle. Taking on too much at once probably means that you will drop everything as it may become too much to sustain.

Every time you make progress along the way, take a moment to tune in to your B.B.C., use your breath and your physical gesture to anchor your clearing. As you do, you are recording progress, success and gratitude in your neurobiology. Gratitude is one of the fastest creative energies you can harness. As you teach these new states to your mind-emotion-body receptors, it strengthens your ability to connect to your internal resources rapidly, and when you need them most. This will come in handy when you have a 'low-energy day'. Recording these states in your neurobiology enables you to build mental, emotional and physical resilience.

Resilience with NeuroBiology Reprogramming™

Case Study—Trevor

Trevor's Wheel

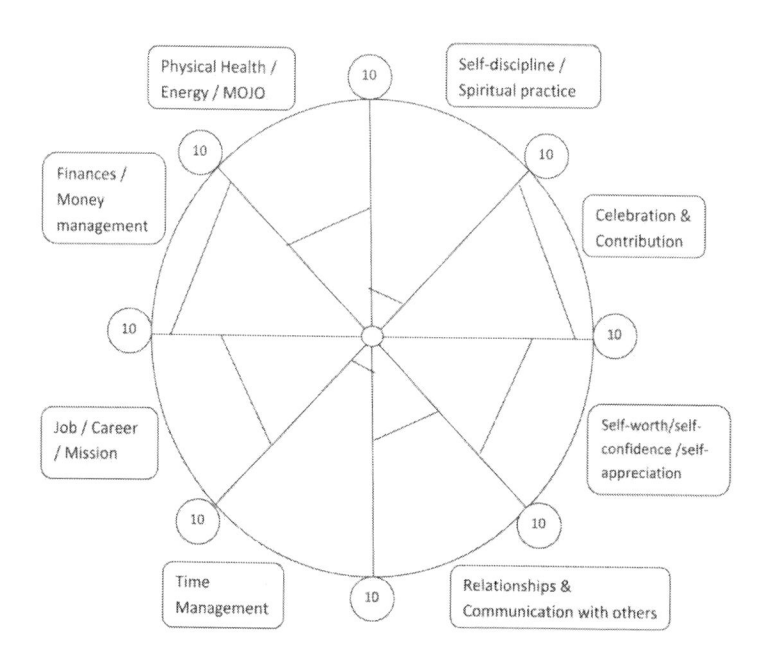

In the example above, Trevor's wheel looks as follows:
- Physical Health / Energy / MOJO: 5
- Self-discipline / Spiritual practice: 2
- Celebration & Contribution: 9
- Self-worth / self-confidence / self-appreciation: 7
- Relationships & Communication with others: 4
- Time Management: 1

- Job / Career / Mission: 6
- Finances / Money management: 9

When Trevor looked at his finished wheel, he figured that the Relationships & Communication area would automatically improve if he managed his time better. He hoped that this would eventually free up his mind, so he could invest some in himself.

When we began working together, I proposed that Trevor look at his 'Job / Career / Mission' area as this was undoubtedly linked to his 'Self-worth / self-confidence / self-appreciation', because one feeds into the other. Through collaborative conversation, it became clear to him that he held many beliefs and unspoken assumptions right there. He was able to clear them out without much resistance. Seeing the benefits he created for himself gave him a surge of self-confidence in his own abilities, and re-energised his sense of purpose and potential instantly. He found that this naturally fed into his 'Physical Health / Energy / MOJO', which made it easier for him to keep on practising. It also allowed him to access clearer thinking, which consolidated his self-confidence.

Regaining self-confidence contributed to his sense of presence, and he found it easier to communicate with his partner. As a mutual conversation opened, it restored verbal intimacy, which brought them closer.

EXERCISE—PART 2
Identify the Programs/Beliefs

Now that you have identified what areas of your life you would like to work on, it is time to clear the beliefs attached to them. This exercise is designed to help you recognise the programmes, or unspoken assumptions, that are in the way so you can begin to make room for the new. You may have several areas you would like to work on, but please treat one at a time. Once you have done it once, you can use the same process again for another topic. Use the whole process as is outlined below for each area.

My chosen area to work on, develop or take to the next level is:

-
-
-

1.   Why do you absolutely want and need to make that change? Write 3 good reasons:

1.

2.

3.

When you know why it can work, tune in to your B.B.C. and use your physical gesture to anchor the decision, this state of knowing—certainty.

2. Write 1-3 beliefs why it may not work:

1.

2.

3.

Note: These are the beliefs, the programmes, in your subconscious mind that are in the way of your potential. Use your DELETE key to clear them, or 'I release you from . . .' When done, take a breath and use your physical gesture to anchor this state of peace, relief or clarity.

3. Write 3 concrete steps you are willing to take to close the gap between where you are right now and what you want to create/experience:

1.

2.

3.

4. Set a date to begin taking the 1-3 steps you wrote above. This is an agreement with yourself; don't break it! (Please set a day and make a note of it in your diary / phone / electronic calendar so you show up. If you have to cancel for any reason, have enough respect for yourself to reschedule in the same way you would with a good friend.)

Date for step 1:

Date for step 2:

Date for step 3:

5. What consequences do you expect will happen if you don't follow up on your decision?

-

-

-

6. What do you need to eliminate from your life right now to help create the results you want?

1.

2.

3.

7. What are 1-3 situations you ABSOLUTELY CANNOT change, that you need to make peace with?

1.

2.

3.

8. Think about one area that is working fantastically well for you right now, and outline 3 reasons why it does so:

1.

2.

3.

9. Can you use the same beliefs and energy from question 8 to improve or take what you want to the next level?

- Yes, because

- No, because

LET'S TALK STORY!

More Humorous Sufi Wisdom from our Friend Nasruddin

One late evening, a passer-by finds Nasruddin absorbed and preoccupied on the side of the road.

'Mullah, pray tell me: what is wrong?'

'Ah, my friend, I seem to have lost my keys. Would you help me search for them? I know I had them when I left the tea house.'

The passer-by helps Nasruddin with the search for the keys. The man is searching here and there for quite some time, but no keys are to be found. He looks over to Nasruddin and finds him searching around the small area lit up by a street lamp.

'Mullah, why are you only searching there?'

'Why would I search where there is no light?'

CHAPTER 6—PRACTICE RECAP

TAKING NEUROBIOLOGY REPROGRAMMING™ ON THE ROAD

2-PART EXERCISE

Part One: How smooth is your ride? Use 'The Wheel of Life' diagram to gain insight as to where you are right now, and to decide what area you want to work on or take to the next level.

Part Two: Identify the beliefs—the programmes and unspoken assumptions—that are keeping you from accessing your inherent potential in these areas. Apply the full NeuroBiology Reprogramming™ method to begin clearing layers of limiting beliefs, conscious and subconscious, and to develop resilience in that area. This will allow you to access some more of your potential.

CHAPTER 7

NEUROBIOLOGY REPROGRAMMING™

LEVEL TWO: EMOTIONAL RESILIENCE

"Life shrinks or expands in proportion to one's courage."

— Anaïs Nin

On your way to ultimate resilience, and having got a grasp on how to develop mental resilience, our next frontier is emotional resilience.

In this chapter, you will learn about emotional intelligence and gain emotional resilience. This means that you will be able to develop self-mastery in your mind-emotions capacity, and have a handle on its process.

Having emotional resilience as well as emotional intelligence is important because one may be 'emotionally intelligent' and yet remain tied to a life-long, repeating pattern or be at the mercy of what I call an emotional 'default setting'. If this is the case, feelings and ideas like 'It's just the way it is' or 'This is who I am' can drain much emotional resilience, as these are extremely self-depreciating.

Any recurrent emotions anyone may have is an echo from a belief that is embedded in the subconscious mind, hence, the difficulty of getting to it. Yet, these emotions provide us with the perfect pointer, the direction in which we can angle our clearing tools.

In this chapter, the step we will use to develop emotional resilience is the same as the one we used for mental resilience. However, some knowledge about the emotional body will do much to alleviate many misunderstandings as to its uses and capacity.

Can Anyone Control Their Emotions?

We briefly touched on the subject of emotions earlier on, and I shared with you that trying to control emotions is neither possible, beneficial, productive, nor realistic. I also mentioned that no one can control anyone else's emotions, nor respond favourably to external orders about 'controlling' one's own emotions.

Did you ever tell someone to 'calm down' when they were agitated? Or did someone ever tell you 'relax!' when you were irritated? You remember how that felt? Not exactly productive or beneficial, I think you will agree. Ordering or controlling emotions simply doesn't work, not on ourselves or anyone else. However, we can certainly choose different thoughts, which will immediately and effectively change the emotions we feel.

Let's say that you are attempting to help someone move through difficult emotions. The best course of action would be to simply offer different thoughts, so the person you are dealing with can begin to *feel* differently. If you have children, you will have already used this simple method, rather than order them to stop crying, for example. You may have simply diverted their attention to something else. Here is a novel idea: do this on yourself! It works.

The following is a brief description of how emotions are usually handled, or mishandled to be more accurate. These have the power to create real pain, much unnecessary suffering, and drain your resilience.

Emotions are usually:

- Being indulged in and taken as a lasting truth, allowing them to grow out of proportion for indefinite amounts of time.
- Being ignored, which means that they gain momentum. This can create problems that are more serious than their origin, like feeling disconnected, which means that we are actually becoming disconnected. Feeling that no one or and nothing can help us is a dangerous path to follow.
- Repressed or denied, which means they get condensed in physical tissue and create stress and illnesses in the physical body.

None of these options are conducive to living a fulfilling life or accessing any peace of mind. This means that resilience is at an all-time low, and that some serious measures, in terms of daily self-discipline, need to be applied.

This is essential because emotions are the centrepiece and the link in our internal mechanism of creation.

Take a moment to see the following diagram and note the functions and uses of the emotional body.

A Diagram of You

The Mechanism of Internal and External Creation

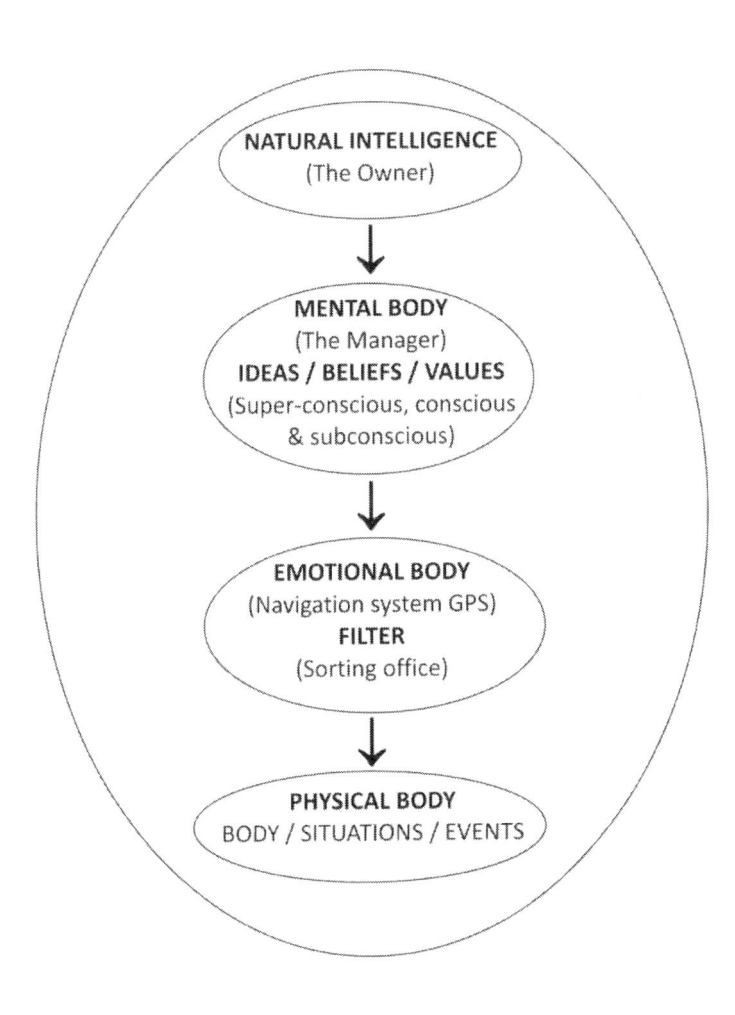

NATURAL INTELLIGENCE
(The Owner)

↓

MENTAL BODY
(The Manager)
IDEAS / BELIEFS / VALUES
(Super-conscious, conscious
& subconscious)

↓

EMOTIONAL BODY
(Navigation system GPS)
FILTER
(Sorting office)

↓

PHYSICAL BODY
BODY / SITUATIONS / EVENTS

NATURE OF EMOTIONS

Emotions are one of our three attributes. They are the connective element between our mental body and our physical body. Whether we are aware of them or not, emotions are always there, contributing to everything we do, reflecting the reason why we do it, and influencing how we do it.

Emotions are a crucial link between our other two attributes, the mental and the physical bodies. They determine whether the thoughts we entertain—both conscious and subconscious—can actually get actualised and create tangible results or not. They also determine the nature of our experience. This is depicted by the downward arrows in the diagram. This means that emotions have the power to define our state of health and energy, and play a huge part in the results we get in our endeavours: our projects, our career, our relationships, our money-making ability, the opportunities we create for ourselves, etc.

Until trained, the mind runs the show and very much runs riot with repetitive, self-deprecating beliefs, which means that equivalent emotions follow. This is what I call the mind-emotion tyrannical duo. For the most part, this mental dialogue is focused on thoughts of fear and lack, and in the worst case scenario, self-hatred. This is when we think that every thought we entertain is a reality set in stone, which of course, produces matching emotions. But none of that is true, or at least, not unless we want it to be. We already know that each thought is only a probability. The questions is: is it complementary to you, or not?

The effect of an untamed mind-emotions process is to create and recreate the same challenges so we might finally become aware of them, and do something about transforming them. The way this materialises itself is often through an external situation or a person with whom we may be dealing. This is precisely why it can look like what is going on 'out there' is nothing to do with us. This illusion is the origin of blame and the cause of some the pain we may feel. Yet, one of the main purposes of the reality we contribute to is to realise how we are affecting it with every thought, emotion, and action we take. This gives us a chance to experience it and enjoy it, or gives us a chance to change it. In both cases, it reflects our human potential.

You are a Master-Creator. Don't ever forget it!

ATTRIBUTES OF THE EMOTIONAL BODY

Let's explore each analogy given for the emotional body, so you can appreciate its awesome capacity.

GPS

The emotional body is very much like your own, built-in navigation system, or GPS. This means that it really is a fantastic asset, and just like a GPS, it gives you a sensory depiction of your thoughts—both conscious and subconscious—via your feelings. Basically, it allows you to get a sense of what is going on around you much before it reaches conscious mind computation.[16] This is because the subconscious mind is directly linked to the emotional body, which means that it by-passes the conscious level.

For example, Applied Kinesiology is a method that allows the therapist to get answers straight from the subconscious, through muscle-testing, using body wisdom. This insures a much clearer and more accurate answer than if it had been analysed or rationalised by the conscious mind.

The Heart Is King

We are much more than the eye can see. There is a large field of electromagnetic energy all around our body. This can be scientifically demonstrated today, as we live in amazing times where science and spirituality are merging for the first time, ever. Our brain and heart have their own electrical and magnetic fields. The heart is known today as the only organ that sends more information to the brain than the brain sends to it. This is far reaching, and can explain some of the healings that have taken place; although, these were thought to be impossible, due to an area of the brain that may have been damaged beyond repair.

The heart detects much energy-based information

---

[16] *The User Illusion: Cutting Consciousness Down to Size* by Tor Nørretranders

that is produced both inside us and all around us, and informs the brain of it through these electrical and magnetic currents. In fact, the heart is recognised today as the 'first brain' and there is some wonderful work and research worth looking at on this subject.[17] You can bring yourself to a state of calm and harmony by simply putting a hand on your heart and taking a few conscious breaths, just the same way we use the B.B.C. This facilitates a state that is known as 'coherence' between the brain and the heart. This is a simple self-healing technique you can do anytime, which will certainly replenish your emotional and even physical resilience level the moment you do it.

The Gut is Where Your True Direction Lies

We take in information below conscious level all the time. We can only be consciously aware of a fraction of what we register, as we have seen when we studied the mind. [Conscious mind processes 14 bits of information per second while the subconscious mind processes 20 million[18] in the same second.]

Another way we process information below the conscious or 'intellectual level' is through our 'gut feeling'. The physical location for this gut feeling is between our ribcage and our stomach, at the site of our solar plexus. As an entrepreneur, this is an absolutely invaluable tool to harness, refine and listen to. It can

---

[17] Take a look at the Heart Math Institute.

[18] *The User Illusion: Cutting Consciousness Down to Size* by Tor Nørretranders

allow us access to valuable information that cannot be perceived with our other traditional five senses: hearing, seeing, smelling, tasting, and touching. This GPS can help us to know how to take each new step forward, and in what direction. This can be valuable in business if we need resilience, particularly if there are no obvious or physical signs of success... yet! This makes up part of the 80% internal wiring. This can mean make or break.

Although I haven't yet had the honour or the pleasure to meet Sir Richard Branson, I feel that I can venture out and say that he is quite familiar with using his GPS or gut feeling. It undoubtedly gave him the entrepreneurial courage and edge to take his enterprise off the ground—no pun intended!—leaving many hesitant competitors behind.

Once you have all the 'structural and financial' information you may need to make a particular decision, you will derive much benefit from listening in to your own guidance. This information is translated as a physical sensation so you can actually become aware it, via your gut feeling. I cannot think of one entrepreneur I have talked to who does not listen to their gut feeling, even if they don't know what it is! They still use it.

Your Built-In Alarm System

Another function of the emotional body is that it can act as your own internal alarm system. The emotional body is an expression of the subconscious mind, and can therefore give us a signal—via our feelings—of an impending threat, both internal and external. This can be invaluable for personal safety, particularly if you choose to listen to it, and act accordingly. You may have paid a price whenever you ignored your gut feeling, having opted to listen to 'intellectual reasoning' instead, only to suffer the consequences. We have all done that at various times, which is part of our training for finding out what truly amazing built-in attributes we have, and how to make use of them. This is always a haphazard experience until you know what it is and how to use it. I wholeheartedly hope that you didn't have to pay too high a price for your training.

FILTER
The emotional body is like a 'sorting office'

Different emotions lead to different results, both in our own state of health and energy, and in what actions and, therefore, what results we can create. In this way, our emotions very much act as 'a filter' or 'a sorting office', effectively selecting what is possible for us, and what is not.

Thoughts + Emotions = Feelings

Feelings = Beliefs = Determines what steps are taken = What success can be achieved

Our emotions literally work as a 'triage mechanism' that pre-selects what we are able to create, both internally, in terms of state of health and energy, and externally, in the outcome produced. This includes all business concerns, investments, or any other dealings to which we are committed.

Luxury or Hindrance?

The emotions also allow us to benefit from a 'buffer of time' that gives a chance to literally *change our mind*. In other words, there is a lapse of time between thoughts and physical results. Although we usually let impatience set in, particularly when results don't show up immediately, or within the time frame we planned, this 'buffer of time' can actually be a luxury, and in some cases, a life-saver. It gives us the opportunity to course-correct our thinking, to clear what mindset does not serve a particular purpose or intended goal, and allows us to harness new and more profitable ideas, if we want to use business moves as an example.

Example: Let's say that you are experiencing difficulties in your business or department right now, and that you are declaring:

'We are not going to make it.'

(**Note:** This could be applied to your relationship, or anywhere you are encountering serious challenges.) How do you FEEL when you say this? Disappointed, frustrated, fearful, sad, angry? All the above? What kind of words are you going to tell your business partner(s). What are your clients going to feel? What kind of energy will be behind the service/product you are offering? What actions will you take, feeling this way, and what results will you get by entertaining a feeling of 'defeat'?

You may already be familiar with the concept of 'energy marketing', which is a form of marketing beyond the traditional means. Businesses are not just businesses, they are literally the projection of someone's mind, and an expression of their belief system, their potential and their resilience level. This is what I call the internal wiring, and as already mentioned, it accounts for an average of 80% of any success. This is precisely why you will benefit most by thinking about your business or your department as an extension of who you are as a person. This will dramatically shift your focus, which will shift your feelings, and with it, drive the actions you must take to make success a more probable outcome.

Now let's use what we have learnt so far, assuming that your preferred choice is success. Begin by applying the DELETE key to the belief 'We are not going to make it'. This statement is based in fear, so you can also mentally say 'I release you from the fear of 'not making it'.' Take a breath, and, no matter how brief, anchor this moment of respite, trust or, if nothing else, emptiness in the absence of fear, with your physical gesture.

Having done the first part, now declare the following:

'Things are very challenging right now, but there are plenty of resources available out there, and I trust my own guidance to find exactly what or who I need to turn this situation around.'

How does it feel when you read these words? Positive? Possible? Probable? Strategic? Resilient? Probably all the above, which is really good news. This will give you the resourcefulness necessary to bring in what you need, and turn things around.

Think Tank

Even though things may be very challenging in the moment, or you may not have the answer just yet, clearing the belief that said 'we are not going to make it' can allow just enough space for a solution to enter the mind. No matter how brief, a little mental space will afford you emotional space, which is the essence of resilience.

Trying to think of a solution while feeling afraid is not a productive exercise, as it can often precipitate making the wrong decision, creating problems more serious than the original challenge. This is because physiologically speaking, fear means that your mind-body is literally flooded with norepinephrine and cortisol, the hormones and neurotransmitters of stress. This is not a good state to access your own capacity to reason calmly or to clearly see your next step, I think you will agree.

Instead, you can use your B.B.C., or if you have a little time and space on your hands, take 2-3 minutes to practice your B.B.M.E., with your eyes closed this time. This is what will allow the overwhelming fear and worry to subside. Using your clearing tools will take care of eliminating the original thought-form that created this particular problem in the first place.

Choosing to use your practices is a smart move, as it is effectively tapping into your 80% internal wiring. This will create the internal space you need, which means that your mind will be more receptive to hearing the answers or the solutions required. It will also clarify your next best step, and give you the resilience you need to achieve it, or to tweak it if necessary. A far cry from giving up.

What Happens in the Worst Case Scenario?

You get to remain at peace, in your most resilient capacity, knowing that you did your very best to resolve the situation at hand. It will save you from falling apart for an undetermined amount of time, and allow you to regroup and re-source, in readiness for a new start, when you will feel ready.

Ultimately, the currency of success is not what we do or what we get, but who we become in the process. Who you are, which includes your personal resilience, is your true inner wealth. This is, and will always be, yours. Everything else is transient.

What Happens in the Best Case Scenario?

This will have been the defining moment that allowed you to change course, use your full potential and create unprecedented results. You will have gained an enormous amount of insight and resilience. There will always be goals and challenges. The real currency of success and wealth, the kind that cannot be taken away, is the development of your internal wiring, which includes personal resourcefulness and your untapped human potential. This is why Benjamin Franklin noted:

> *"An investment in knowledge always pays the best interest."*

THE SCIENCE BEHIND EMOTIONAL RESILIENCE

This Way Down—Handle with Care!

As depicted by the arrow in the diagram, you have learnt that thoughts energise emotions, and the two combined create the beliefs with which you create your results and opportunities.

This effectively means that the emotions are very much a double-edged sword. They can energise thoughts and have positive results when your beliefs are based on a sense of trust, self-reliance, confidence, strategic thinking, and positive anticipation.

They can equally energise negative habitual thinking patterns, fuelled by a lack of self-confidence, nervousness, or fear-based anticipation from past experiences. All of which sets the tone for future experiences. Negative events leave an imprint that is up to 10 times stronger than any positive ones, which will often be completely forgotten. This is because our defence mechanism is set to recognise anything that remotely looks, sounds or feels like a past traumatic event. This is at the base of all emotional trauma, such as phobias and PTSD (post-traumatic stress disorder). While developing the ability to be discerning is very relevant, so we can avoid real stress or danger when we recognise it next time, these reactions cannot be rationalised. This is because they are coming from the information that is imprinted in the subconscious mind, being expressed through the emotional body.

Yet, any emotional signalling can be changed as we clear the thought-forms that are associated with it.

A Quick Dive into Current Science

We live in privileged times, in so far as what you are learning here can be proven with solid scientific findings. Although it was not always that easy, this did not stop visionaries, leading edge creators, thinkers and inventors using this knowledge since the beginning of time. In recent years, neuroscience research has confirmed that the body-mind-emotions is an intricate system that works as a closely bonded community, in constant communication with one another.

Dr. Candace Pert, neuroscientist, provided groundbreaking research showing that emotions influence our cells, and have a direct impact on our physical state of health and energy. She demonstrated how emotions release particular chemicals in our body (the neuropeptides) that act as the 'information substance'[19] that our brain processes. Her conclusion was, 'The body is the unconscious mind'.

Dr. Bruce Lipton, neuroscientist, explains in his work that 'our genes are not pre-deterministic', meaning that they are not 'set in stone' as was commonly believed by science and medicine until recently. He demonstrated that each cell's behaviour is shaped by the information that it receives via its receptors and the environment it lives in. The information that our cells receive is none other than our own thoughts, conscious and subconscious, which form our beliefs, and the environment in which we live. This includes our heart's electric and electromagnetic energy.

This also means that many of the hereditary factors that we once thought to be unavoidable can actually be cleared, and you have the very method to be able to do just that with NeuroBiology Reprogramming™. Dr. Bruce Lipton's research is known as *epigenetic*—a branch of biology. He explains that less than 5% of all illnesses are genetically hereditary,[20] instead of the near 95% that was once accepted. Please note that this has not yet gone into mainstream science, as this will, in

---

[19] See *Molecules of Emotion* by Dr. Candace B. Pert.

[20] *The Biology of Belief* by Dr. Bruce Lipton

time, revolutionise and redefine how we approach illness, and how we treat the body. This is part of the changes we are experiencing.

Dr. Bruce Lipton's findings effectively mean that, if we can change the thoughts we emit, in particular the subconscious ones since they run 95-99% of all our processes, we can literally rewrite our DNA and, with it, our own history. In practical terms, this means we have far more power to affect our state of health and energy, but also, and as is our concern here, our business and our ability to create the kind of success we have in mind. This is groundbreaking!

A Brief Example of How This Works

If Henry repeatedly fears the cancer his father had, the fear is the environment picked up by his cell receptors, messaging his genes with the relevant chemical sequence that will very likely activate the first cancer cell. This fear—in this case, consciously entertained—creates an acidic environment, which is the perfect ground for illness to effectively take root.

In the opposite case, peace, trust, laughter, or gratitude will instruct the body with information that will set the neurotransmitters into action that will promote an alkaline environment. This is the perfect ground for health and well-being. By now, many more people have experienced what is known as spontaneous remission from cancer. Even if they do not know anything about what is described here.

The Power Is in Your Mind-Emotion Connection

Whether you choose to lean on growing scientific research, or prefer to practise the intuitive age-old wisdom of ancient spirituality, the evidence points to the same outcome: the quality of your life depends on the quality of your emotions. The good news is that NeuroBiology Reprogramming™ allows you to deal effectively with fear-based emotions as it did with limiting mindsets. It means that you can literally delete any damaging programme, including fear of all kinds, lack of self-confidence, hereditary illness, poverty, failure, etc. Using this system is a game-changer and, as a consequence, a life-changer.

A miracle is simply a science not yet understood, but when we do, it becomes a technology.

Let's Get Back to Business and Observe How Emotions Can Affect Your Professional Success

Let's say you have all the skills and did all the right things, according to what you learnt in your particular industry sector. According to mainstream thinking, this ought to have guaranteed the success of your business. Yet, you fell short in the results you anticipated. How could that be? You probably had each and every business skill required, and perhaps even completed an MBA!

Most of us were taught in early education that we create our career opportunities solely based on the skills we learn. We were all encouraged to focus on the money-making aspect of our career choices. There was nothing whatsoever taught about learning any kind of personal science, or how to harness our own potential. While the education we received was useful, it completely omitted the all-important fact that a large part of any success is based on our own *internal wiring*.

It turns out that the skill-part of any success is a much smaller part of the equation than anticipated. Personal resilience—*internal wiring*—determines the outcome, and although this is an observation rather than a strict rule, it can account for up to 80% of the success equation. I am alluding to the 80/20 Pareto principle, which works well here to describe that any outcome created in business, can rely on roughly 20% skills and 80% internal wiring.

If you are not familiar with this principle, Vilfredo Pareto was an Italian economist who found that 80% of Italy's wealth belonged to only 20% of the population. This observation has been applied to many more subjects and proven relevant to depict that 80% of the effects come from 20% of the causes. For example, 80% of a company's profits come from 20% of its customers, 20% of the staff produce 80% of the results, 80% of complaints filed toward a company often comes from 20% of its clients, etc.

This means that you may be doing all the right things, and yet lack the self-confidence or personal resilience necessary to keep pushing past the challenges that naturally occur along the way. Eventually, you may simply get tired of it all, feel as though you 'failed', give up, and believe that what you do doesn't have any value. This could strengthen an already existing limiting mindset, such as 'I was never very good at . . .', or 'This is not the right time to . . .'

This is unfortunately the plea of too many. For example, if you associate the word 'failure' with 'the end', this very much heralds the end for your business or your efforts for promotion. The truth is that 'failure' is just another word for a signpost that really means that, although a particular idea may not have worked out the way you planned, you now know to try something else. Think of it as a process of elimination—it is! Success is very much still ahead, and the idea of 'failure' then simply lets you know that you are ONE STEP CLOSER to your goal. As you may have heard before, in the famous quote of Henry Ford:

"Whether you think you can, or you think you can't—you're right."

As already mentioned, businesses are not just businesses, they are an extension of a person's internal wiring, or mind-emotion connection. Most business ideas are good, but the person may lack the 80% internal wiring required to keep pushing beyond challenges, or retooling until progress is regular and steady, and begins to produce the kind of result that make success more certain.

The same goes within any organisation, where the quality of the culture depends on each person that is a part of it. If this is your present work environment, you may have noticed that no amount of employee engagement has solved the deep personal dissatisfaction or frustration that may be prevalent. This is because personal fulfilment and the desire to become more resilient are only effective when they are a personal choice. Job satisfaction is an important factor, particularly if it engages a sense of contribution that is appreciated, but it will not be able to make up for the larger part of the resilience that is required in our professional lives.

The reality is that most people spend hours working at something just to 'pay the bills'. Fewer have the necessary internal wiring to create a venture that combines passion, purpose and income. Even if this is the case, personal resilience comes into play as soon as serious challenges arise, including those that can arise when we need to cope with massive explosive growth.

HOW TO MAKE USE OF THE EMOTIONAL BODY

In the practice of NeuroBiology Reprogramming™, the emotions represent an all-important role or 'cue' to release what holds us up. The emotions are an expression of our subconscious thoughts: the ones that we can never be aware of consciously. While we may never get to the 'bottom of it' in finding out where an old limiting belief came from, we can certainly release its limiting influence.

We have all had the experience of getting up one morning, with everything being structurally equal to the day previous, and yet feeling inexplicably troubled, for no apparent reason. These are times where the emotions give us a clue to DELETE some unconscious thought-forms that are replaying. We may 'think' we know where they are coming from, but closer to the truth is we cannot, as these will already be the result of a previous event. Remember, 20 million bits of information per second... since we came into existence! We are the product of a long family lineage.

If you have a family programme that you find useful and complementary to the development of your potential, you can keep it, or even use it to enjoy a feeling of gratitude. You can breathe it in whenever you think of it, anchor it, and it will keep on bringing you opportunities and events charged with the same energy.

You may also choose to clear a good program, which will allow an inspired and upgraded version of it to be experienced.

For anything else that keeps you trapped and limited, doubtful, worried, or feeling small, do yourself a favour and just DELETE it.

*It is tempting to have an external reason for the depression, dissatisfaction or disappointment anyone may feel inside,
but the fact is that these show up because they are long-term unconscious thought-forms,*

*emitting a signal via the emotional body,
so they can finally be released . . . that is all! There is no
other purpose for any of these feelings.*

Even in the case of feeling happy or joyful, if your happiness relies on external events or people, you are dependent on them for your good feelings, and are therefore at their mercy. A bind that is hard to break.

No Denial, Just Opportunities

When you feel a particular emotion, you may of course acknowledge the message that may be included with it. If you find that there is something that needs to be addressed, do so in the moment, or as soon as possible so it is most relevant, and effective. Once you have dealt with it, clear it, which will allow you to let it go. You cannot keep serving up the past, or seeing with the eyes of the past and not suffer or remain stuck in the present.

Sometimes there are no hidden messages in your emotions, other than an old emitting signal from something that is long gone, and cannot even be remembered. This, like the rest of the limiting thoughts and emotions, is best cleared out. A limiting emotion such as resentment, fear or depression, for example, is a signal letting you know that the time has come for you to free yourself from an old belief. You won't necessarily know what the belief is, so you can use the DELETE clearing tools whenever that particular emotion surfaces.

As you read this, your mind may be telling you that this doesn't make sense; for example, this may sound too simple a treatment for self-deprecating emotions. Be aware that this thought, if you are having it, is one of the programmes in place that can keep you from attempting to free yourself. It is possible to be addicted to one's own suffering, as suffering can provide a sensation in itself, better than the numbness that may be experienced.

Personal suffering can also be a crutch in itself, as this may be the way that we receive attention and energy from other people, in the form of pity or concern, for example. It is liberating to realise that, as we choose to clear our own beliefs, you can have a better connection with the people around you. We don't have to hold on to any crutches.

APPLYING NeuroBiology Reprogramming™ TO THE EMOTIONAL BODY

In all simplicity, and to develop a significant amount of personal resilience, you can do the following:

1. Cultivate the emotions that are complementary to your well-being and expansion. Gratitude, for example, is such an emotion. You can decide to be grateful by simply thinking about something small that brings you gratitude. When you feel it, take a breath and anchor it with your physical

gesture. This entrains your neurobiology with a positive habit. Gratitude benefits you, your family and your immediate world: your department or your business. This is one way you can *leave a profit* wherever you go and with whatever endeavour to which you are committed. It will also make it more likely that you are met with the same kind of energy, although this is not the aim.

2. Be willing to release or DELETE the emotions that are repetitive and self-deprecating. They are coming from some conscious or unconscious repeating thoughts. These are literally crowding your subconscious mind, reducing your resilience level, and disabling you from accessing your potential and resourcefulness in the moment.

With daily use, NeuroBiology Reprogramming™ can become a subconscious habit. It is like anything else you once learned. You consciously repeated it enough times that it became a learned habit, like walking, driving, counting, spelling, etc. When NeuroBiology Reprogramming™ is second nature to you, you will find that you can deal with absolutely anything, and remain at peace, knowing how to get into action from a place of resourcefulness, rather than a fear-based reaction. This is your birthright. This is effectively developing self-mastery and bulletproof resilience.

EXERCISE
Where Do You Live Emotionally?

Having just explored the impact of emotions, and how they are the fuel that powers up beliefs into tangible results, let's make use of it for you. Please take a moment to revisit what area you want to work on, based on the result you got in your Wheel of Life.

As a brief review regarding the use of your emotions, it is as simple as harnessing the good ones and deleting the ones that are causing you restriction, pain or limitation.

The following self-inquiry exercise is designed to help you gain insight and realise what your predominant emotional 'thermostat' is, in the area you want to improve or transform. This will help you to understand the nature of the results you are creating, and allow you to clear and change your perceptions so you can create the desired results. It will also give you the foresight necessary to re-energize plans and goals you may have given up on. If nothing else, you will be able to live in peace, knowing how to handle your own emotions.

The list below outlines some options from the vast spectrum that is available to us, in terms of emotions and feelings. This list is by no means exhaustive, so you can add to it if you notice that some of your emotions are not listed. However, the list does begin and end with what I find is the most important, which is for you to realise whether you are mostly feeling empowered or disempowered. If you are not feeling empowered, you will be able to use the clearing tools included to free yourself from what influences are holding you up, so you can move closer to the side of empowerment.

When you look through the list, you might like to define what emotions you usually entertain at work, when you get home at night, and on weekends.

An extension of the same exercise: When you work up the courage for it, and when you can solidly rely on using NeuroBiology Reprogramming™ to remain empowered, you can ask your spouse and children the same question: what emotions are you predominantly radiating when you are at home? You may find that other family members want to play this game with you.

Years ago, I used this with my own teenagers. They loved being able to tell me when I was grumpy, not present or loving enough! This naturally opened the conversation, and allowed for clarity, honesty, vulnerability in the right environment. Sometimes it meant having a lot of fun, and, yes, the agreement was reversible! Please don't forget to keep light-hearted and humorous with what you hear.

"The truth might set you free, but it will probably piss you off first!" — Joe Klaas

At this time in my life, I mostly feel:

1. Empowered
2. Inspired
3. Peaceful
4. Free
5. Joyous
6. Grateful
7. Loving
8. Passionate
9. Excited
10. Enthusiastic
11. Energetic
12. Motivated
13. Proud
14. Courageous
15. Daring
16. Eager
17. Determined
18. Confident
19. Happy
20. Elated
21. Optimistic
22. Receptive
23. Secure
24. Trusting
25. Contented
26. Satisfied
27. Glad
28. Relieved
29. Bored
37. Impatient
38. Frustrated
39. Overwhelmed
40. Disappointed
41. Confused
42. Suspicious
43. Foolish
44. Inadequate
45. Worried
46. Entitled
47. Arrogant
48. Blaming
49. Ashamed
50. Discouraged
51. Bitter
52. Frustrated
53. Empty
54. Bereft
55. Grieving
56. Hatred
57. Raging
58. Angry
59. Jealous
60. Unhappy
61. Insecure
62. Shocked
63. Guilty
64. Lost
65. Insignificant

30. Lonely
31. Miserable
32. Weepy
33. Sad
34. Pessimistic
35. Upset
36. Irritated

66. Worthless
67. Self-loathing
68. Fearful
69. Desperate
70. Depressed
71. Powerless
72. Disempowered

Note: First of all, and most importantly, there is no right or wrong with emotions and feelings. All of them are 'passing probabilities', and as we already learned earlier on, none of them are who you are at the core. So they cannot define you unless you say so.

The ones that are good can be magnified and the ones that are not so good are the doorway through which you can liberate yourself. Think of this as a win-win situation! No matter how old, repetitive or at the forefront any emotion may be, it can be used to transform your life. This is a personal guarantee. Don't forget that you can get a break from any emotion by simply using your B.B.M.E., so you can rest as your Inner Being, or conscious awareness, which is who you are at the core. This is always just one breath away.

Consider your emotions to be just like shades on a pallet with choices of many different colours. In this particular case, you are the artist. The colours are your emotions, and the painting is the life you are designing with every thought and feeling, each breath you take and step you make.

The next thing to remember is that everything

changes, no matter how bad or how great it is in the moment. The only unwavering aspect of who you are that doesn't change is your Inner Being, and your creative ability. You can choose to experience yourself as what you want to be or do, as your potential is truly limitless. Grasping and holding onto anything, even if it is good, is often limiting, creating boredom at best. Common programmes that are embedded in our subconscious mind are sayings like 'Better the devil you know than the devil you don't know'. What a shame it is to choose to reduce ourselves to such a poor choice 'devil or devil' when we are unlimited beings, who can create from ideas alone. This programme is the kind of thinking that can stop a business from growing and thriving. It comes from fear, limitation, hesitation, lack of courage, playing 'small'; none of which can produce compounding success.

Reminiscing over past achievements always robs us of how new and magnificent our present moment could be. The list above is only designed to help you see where you stand at this time, so you can have direction toward what emotions to delete. While you will often not be able to know what beliefs are creating the painful emotions you keep on feeling, you can certainly use these same emotions as your cue to let go of them by using 'I release you from . . . (name the emotion)'.

You don't need to know how electricity works to switch on the light and enjoy seeing better.
What matters is that you use the switch to free yourself.

The same goes for the emotions that are in the way of your accessing more of your resilience and personal power. You don't need to know where the problem originally came from to delete it. What counts is that you used the DELETE key.

The step to use is the same as we used to clear a limiting mindset, except that here, it is the limiting emotions we are clearing. Because the emotions are a translation of what subconscious beliefs we hold but cannot see, it works equally well as with the beliefs. This is particularly useful when you don't 'feel right', although there is nothing that you can think or see that you find upsetting or debilitating. Unless this is your gut feeling relating something important to you, which you will feel in your gut, these are most probably the deeper programmes.

As mentioned earlier on, if you feel that the emotions you are feeling are conveying some precious information that you need to act upon, go right ahead. Please use your own common sense to decide. Listening to your gut feeling will also reveal much as to whether this is just yours to clear, or if there is really something going on that you must address at once. If this is the case, addressing the problem immediately or as soon as possible will prevent blame and resentment from 'festering' and building momentum, creating more damage.

So when you have circled a self-depreciating emotion from the list above, that may be your 'default setting', or a long-standing one that you want to clear, address your subconscious with the name you already chose, or use 'Jade'.

- Think, say or see the DELETE key (in your own colour) to release the emotional grip you are experiencing. You don't need to know what belief is linked to it. All you need to do to be willing to get free is to consciously apply the DELETE key.

- Once done, take a conscious breath and use your physical gesture to anchor this new wiring.

OR

o Mentally say, 'Jade, I release you from jealousy, anger, blame, resentment, victim-hood, suspicion, etc.' or any other emotions with which you are wrestling.

o Once done, take a conscious breath and use your physical gesture to anchor this new wiring.

Note: Once you have done a clearing, just keep moving with your day. Don't stay sitting down expecting change; it doesn't work that way. Involve yourself with the world, and forget about the clearing you just did. I suggest that you get used to clearing beliefs 'on the go' and as they arise.

DELETE any of the following programmes if they

come up: 'expectation', 'impatience', 'doubt', etc. This is how you are going to create fast and effective change, and you will notice most of it more clearly as you look back, in hindsight, if the occasion calls for it.

The best and most common scenario is that you actually forget you even had a problem, or it seems that you couldn't possibly have been stuck with that particular feeling for so long! This is when things are getting really easy and fun, and your resilience is at its best.

Your Emotional Thermostat

You may notice that you probably harbour 2-3 usual emotions most of the time. I call these emotions your 'emotional thermostat', and that thermostat has a particular 'default setting'. This 'default setting' is an analogy to represent the most familiar emotion(s) that you revert to whenever something happens to you. The external situation and events may vary, but your emotional response is the same. You may have realised that it takes very little for you to feel that particular emotion. The reason that it seems a disproportionate reaction is simply because it is your 'default setting', your long-standing learned response. This is usually something you registered as a child, before the age of 7, as is most of the programming that I come across in my clients and students. Any beliefs perceived to be taken in later are already a consequence of that early programming. It usually just reinforces it.

Using the step given here will disengage that

particular setting, as it will take care to clear the original thought-form that created it. You can consider this emotion to have acted as an 'inner bully' until now, as the person holding this particular emotion suffers most directly from it. Once it is identified, however, it can be re-allocated the title of 'ally'. Why ally? Because it is very simply your reminder to use your DELETE key, since you will have already had enough internal awareness to recognise it. Using the B.B.C. will have helped to identify it in the first place. Soon enough, the emotional charge will be cleared, and you will no longer react in the same way.

Let's use an example.

Case Study—Daniel

Daniel is an entrepreneur. He has been running a new business for the past four years. By the time I met Daniel, his business was going through some serious difficulties, serious enough to look like this business was going to close down. He was experiencing familiar feelings of loss of self-confidence and disappointment, linked to the lack of success in the business.

Although this was not the first time it happened, he had been as diligent as could be and had carried out a business report of current problems, as well as an 'autopsy' of his previous businesses, to try and understand where and why they failed. Like many in a similar situation, he had looked at the external circumstances, at the exclusion of his own internal wiring.

As Daniel began to use his B.B.C., and his B.B.M.E., he managed to get some clarity, as he found this simple practice useful to creating the mental space he needed. As he practised getting a few moments respite throughout the day, he went on to taking 5 minutes twice a day before he walked back into the family home, to get some time out for himself, and to regroup, using his own resources.

He was able to rapidly identify his own mindset, which was formed when he was a small boy and observed his father losing his business, the family estate, and everything that went with it. He recognised that, each time he started something new, he harboured the same—conscious and subconscious—ideas and feelings. Although he did 'all the right things', and cultivated great enthusiasm at the beginning of each venture, deep down, he realised that some of his recurrent thoughts were that this may not go according to plans, since the last business didn't produce the success he anticipated. He also caught himself thinking things like, 'Even if it did, it might not last without bringing up extreme hardship'. The problem was that, of course, he had the evidence to reinforce these thoughts. This created the 'loop' and the self-fulfilling prophecy, the self-perpetrating cycle he was caught in.

By the time we began working together, Daniel was ready to catch every self-depreciating thought, and turn his 'inner bully' into an 'ally'. His goal was simply to be able to move forward, make new tracks, and aim for financial independence first, then freedom.

Whenever Daniel felt frustration or doubt, he simply used the following.

(All names have been changed to preserve confidentiality and privacy.) He chose the name 'Caesar' for his subconscious, to reflect the tremendous courage and dignity he knew he had within himself.

- 'Caesar, I release you from frustration and doubt.'

- As he experienced a few seconds of relief and internal peace, he took a breath in to circulate these feelings in his body, and anchored it with his chosen physical gesture.

AND

- Throughout his busy day, anytime he noticed these two programmes showing up, he simply mentally applied his DELETE key (he chose bright red). He noted that this created an instant space in his mind, which gave him confidence and strength in his own ability to access his own resourcefulness immediately.

- He used a quick conscious breath and his physical gesture to anchor his new state of peace.

- Before long, he felt so empowered that he often felt gratitude. No matter how small an achievement it seemed, he anchored this feeling in his neurobiology by taking a deep breath and using his chosen, physical gesture.

This had the effect of literally depositing 'golden energy' in his resilience bank account.

Armed with his 'internal toolbox', Daniel found it almost effortless to make new decisions, decisions that finally created the success he had once intended. He was able to take some—calculated—risks, which proved to him that his gut feeling was a powerful attribute when combined with his skills.

In fact, one of his comments to me was, 'Where have I been all this time, and why is this information not available mainstream?' His investment in himself began to pay very large, very steady and very regular dividends. His personal life, needless to say, went through the roof as he regained full confidence in himself.

Realising the impact that his family lineage had on him, he also included some clearings regarding the upbringing of his children. They enjoy a very close bond and some heartfelt communication today.

Trust or Fear?

Although the list of emotions and feelings was quite long, they could all be listed under two main headings: trust and fear. Not all fear is incapacitating, however, and we will explore the three different types shortly.

Now that you have a good idea of your internal mechanism of creation, as per the diagram we are using, you can appreciate the effects that thoughts and emotions have on you and your life as a whole.

For example, when we develop trust in ourselves, it is much easier to feel confident, to have self-esteem, to feel more grateful and more appreciative, all of which, of course, creates more of the same as a consequence. The law of cause and effect is always at play. The more trust we have in ourselves, the more relaxed we can afford to be, knowing that we have the internal and external awareness—the foresight—to recognise challenges before they close in on us. This can allow us to change course if and when necessary, or at the very least to be prepared, and be as resourceful and as resilient as possible.

Fear, however, is a very powerful programme, and can be very disempowering. Most of us already hold a huge amount of it disguised as lack of self-esteem, lack of self-confidence, or feelings of 'not being enough' or not being 'loveable enough', which were all imprinted from an early age. I find that 99% of the people I have worked with were still holding some form of these particular two programmes, no matter how wealthy or accomplished. It means that one or two areas of their lives are in serious deficit. But that is okay because we have the tools here to get this cleared.

To add to this, we register an amount of fear-based programming on a daily basis, for example, in the news we hear in the mass media. Let's face it, unless you look in the sports section for your favourite—winning—team, the daily news is, for the most part, bad! There is actually plenty of good news stories, but you won't find those in the mass media. The effect of any fear dilutes our personal power and feeds into already existing fears. When we are afraid, we are more gullible, more controllable. Remember 'better the devil you know'? This is a stifling idea for most things!

But what happens when you are not afraid? You are powerful, opened to solutions, able to create amazing results. Worry is a form of fear; although, it is milder in effect, it is more constant. It can certainly erase our confidence and resilience little by little each day. Most people worry constantly about one thing or another, in case 'lack' shows up, when there is plenty all around. Knowing what you know now, you can understand that 'worry' is pretty much like praying repeatedly for things to go wrong. It is effectively a waste of powerful, mental energy that doesn't help anyone, least of all the person doing the worrying.

Instead of worrying about a particular situation, you can choose to remain aware and alert, calm and trusting your own resources, so you can take action if and when it is called for. This will ensure that you will be far more powerful if you need to act, which does not require 'worry energy'.

Let's have a look at three types of fear, and how to deal with them.

The 3 Types of Fear

As much as we think that our problems are uniquely difficult or different, they are actually always rooted in the same concerns: FEAR. Within fear itself, there are 3 different kinds, that I have labelled them types A, B and C.

Type A Fear—Real Fear
This is the hair-raising feeling in the body that signals imminent and very real danger. The fight-or-flight response takes over the body and allows us to steer ourselves to safety.

Type B F.E.A.R.—False Events Appearing Real
This is a psychological, imagined fear, also known as negative anticipation. While fear can come from a variety of causes, there is a large amount of this type of fear that many of us have in common. As previously mentioned, we learned a large part of these responses from events or interactions we witnessed before the age of 7 years old, below conscious level. These are usually linked to something we observed in our parents, grandparents or the people who raised us. These powerful impressions imprinted many of the responses we have today in the form of the particular programmes we hold. Sometimes, we have gone to the opposite of what we experienced, as to not recreate it.

These fears are:
- The 'fear of lack of . . .', even though you may have plenty of everything you need.
- The 'fear of not being enough', even though you may be accomplished.
- The 'fear of not be loved', even though you may have a life-long partner in your life.
- The 'fear of being rejected' can keep you from meeting a love interest, or keeping it, or from thriving in business, in your career, etc.

The way we operate in our personal and professional relationships, and what we can create in our life very often depends on these primal fears. Have a look to see if any of these are in the way of improving your selected areas of improvement, in the Wheel of Life exercise 'How Smooth Is Your Ride'.

Type C FEAR—Fear as Your Evolutionary Driver

This is the fear of moving beyond where you are/how far you have gotten so far. This type of fear comes up when you are facing new challenges, and with it, perhaps the familiar feeling of 'not wanting to rock the boat', or 'being glad enough to be where you are, so let's not push it!'

Yet this fear presents itself as the challenges that you have at least co-produced—albeit probably unconsciously—so you could grow beyond the occasion, and with it, access some of your untapped potential. This is precisely the time when you need to blow past your own limitations, and take new decisions followed by massive action steps. This is what will insure that you raise yourself or your business to the next level.

However, this can be tricky because when fear is present, it can be hard to distinguish what kind we are facing, as the neurochemicals that are set into motion can make it hard to focus and make the right decision. If you don't realise this, this type of challenge can look like it cannot and must not be surmounted. Yet, this type of fear is your friend, your ally, your teacher, beckoning you to expand and grow into your full potential. In fact, just because you have so much potential, you will co-create occasions that will bring up this type of fear periodically, so that you can keep on growing. Now, remember that there is nothing static, so your business, if we take this as an example, is either growing or shrinking.

Dealing with Type A Fear

When this hair-raising kind of fear comes upon you, your reaction is everything. If you are really at threat, you will find that 'something beyond you' has taken over to steer you to safety. This is your subconscious mind taking over. This is the same mechanism that makes your hand withdraw when it comes too close to a flame, or makes your whole body jump up if you inadvertently sit on a thumbtack. There is little to no input from the conscious mind during such situations.

You may have heard about something similar in the

case where an ordinary passer-by turns into a superhero, running up a stairway on fire to rescue a helpless victim stuck on the third floor of a building in flames. Upon being asked why they did it, they admitted not thinking about it twice, they just went up and did it. Amazing!

Dealing with Type B F.E.A.R. and Type C FEAR

Both Type B, 'False Events Appearing Real', and Type C, 'your evolutionary driver', fear can be managed using the 3 steps you learned, the full NeuroBiology Reprogramming™ method. Practising those 3 steps will allow you to develop your internal GPS and keep your anti-virus system up to date, which will enable you to deal with any kind of challenge with maximum resourcefulness and resilience. It doesn't mean that nothing will challenge you again, or that life will be a straight line from now. It does mean that you will have the mental and emotional resilience you need to deal with anything that is going on in your life, without being drained of your courage or robbed of your peace of mind. Let's look at some case studies.

Case Study—Michael

'My employees are inefficient!'

Michael, a leader in an organisation, often complained about his employees. He found them inefficient, lazy, always complaining, and lacking gratitude. When he got home, his wife, who was busy raising three children, often didn't get a chance to do the extra few jobs he had asked her, which irritated and disappointed him further. To top this up, each night he came home, his kids were invariably in front of their PlayStation, barely noticing him, and definitely not volunteering any communication when he made a feeble attempt of it. At a loss, he tried to implement rules and incentives—at the office and at home—none of which worked at all or long term.

Once Michael started to understand his internal wiring, he got to see how he contributed to the situation he faced in his personal and professional life. He included 'blame' and 'irritation' on his list of anchors, as reminders to tune in to his B.B.C. and B.B.M.E. He felt immediate benefit from his practise; although, the state of peace and relief he experienced was a fleeting few seconds at a time. Nevertheless, he found it useful.

Michael had not intentionally avoided considering the possibility that his own mindset or feelings may play a part in his state of health and energy or, even less, in his surroundings. He believed that the problems he encountered were solely exterior elements to be 'fixed'. As we moved through the NeuroBiology Reprogramming™ programme, he took a closer look at the science behind it, and began to read some articles on neuroscience. This helped him to put some of his scepticism aside, and encouraged him to use his DELETE key. He also felt he had nothing to lose, as he had begun to realise that some of the physical symptoms he experienced may be linked to his own state of stress that he felt daily. These included stomach ulcers and an inability to relax or get a full night's sleep without medication. He particularly resonated with the fact that the stress he endured on a daily basis contributed to a seriously acidic environment in his own body.

Within the next few weeks, he experienced a considerable shift, beginning within his own body. As he got used to brief moments of peace, it encouraged him to keep on using his tools, as feeling better is as cumulative as any other state. He found a name for his subconscious that he never shared, as this is meant to remain confidential, a sacred agreement between one's own conscious and subconscious minds.

- Whenever Michael heard himself blame and criticise people around him, he applied his DELETE key (which he chose to be dark blue).

- He asked if he could still delete a thought-form or feeling after it had happened. The answer is yes, it absolutely works, as ultimately, and especially for the work we are doing here, time is a just a construct. In reality, we are always in the present. Applying a clearing after an event still helps to clear it.

- He then took a conscious breath and used his chosen physical gesture to anchor this new wiring in him.

OR

- Sometimes, he addressed his subconscious, and mentally said, 'I release you from 'judgement' and 'frustration'.'

- He then took a conscious breath, and used his chosen physical gesture to anchor this new wiring in him.

Each time that Michael got a little extra clarity, or mental peace, it helped him to increase his practise, and take actual new steps in his life.

From 'Push' to 'Pull'

Michael's leadership style quickly transformed in the organisation. Instead of pushing his team against an unlikely deadline, he began to really listen and take in information, and found out some key elements that allowed him to contribute in a meaningful way. As he accessed different layers of information, the solutions to each problem came pouring in, and a large project with a strict deadline was fully ready ahead of time, allowing him to have one last final look at it before it was finalised.

Although he admits to 'slipping up' at times, Michael is adamant that 'gratitude' has replaced 'blame' more than 90% of the time. He is working to close the gap. He finds it possible to access peace of mind anytime he needs it, simply because he knows what to do and he does it. He readily admits that he never thought this would be possible. But Michael is a self-directed man, and he had decided that, just like everywhere else in his life, he would make this method work for him, and it did.

With his family, things changed dramatically after he came home one day, asking his kids for feedback on how they had felt about him. He nearly fell off his chair when he heard how they felt, as it was less than complimentary. Very shortly, a new bond was re-established, as communication was made possible, and he gained respect from his kids as they realised that his external toughness masked some vulnerability.

He arranged a special dinner out with his spouse and, when he asked her for feedback, got a similar answer and experience as he did with his kids. The truth was hard to hear but it set them both free, and Marian claims that it saved their marriage.

Although Michael is and will remain a man on a mission, being a self-directed man, he learnt the benefit of communication and presence while he spends time with his family. This freed the household from blame and expectations, as his spouse and his children also realised that it is not the amount of time they spend together that matters most, but the quality and the level of presence that he—and everyone involved—bring into it.

Michael sees his wife with new eyes, and the more he became present with her, the more she opened to him, in ways that he did not even think would be possible. He said that it felt like when they met, only even better. This has strengthened the core of their relationship and deepened the intimacy they share.

Case Study—Ericka

Ericka got angry easily. She got angry anytime she got stuck in traffic, anytime she didn't make the interview for the next promotion at work, the coffee machine got jammed, or she got home and found out that her dog walker left some crumbs on the countertop after eating a sandwich.

Last week she heard from her friend Rachel, who told her that Olivia, a friend of theirs, found out her husband had an affair. Ericka got really mad, as if this had happened to her, by just hearing about it. On the way home that day, Ericka was listening to the news and got irate at the unfairness of the banking system, and worried about her pension fund. A normal day for her, a day like many others.

Ericka suffered from high blood pressure, she was overweight and could not relax. When she tried to rest her legs, they kept on moving as if they had a life of their own. She drank wine most nights, the equivalent of a bottle, but told herself she could stop anytime; although, she didn't feel there was a need to try. She expressed a deep-seated, long-standing dislike for herself. At 39, she was still looking to find a man who she hoped would love her, and with whom she could have at least one child.

While there looked to be so many issues to begin clearing, with the obvious one being a deep-seated anger, it became clear that the bigger programme running at the back of all the other issues was a lack of self-esteem, or self-love. She was convinced that her father had wished she had been a boy, and since she wasn't, he hardly spent any time with her during her childhood. At least that is how she remembers it. She craved his love, which she feels she never got. Instead, she spent her childhood in fear of him, as he had deep-seated anger, and displayed violence around the house, and broke many things. She got hit sometimes, and although she had a younger sister, she took the blame for anything that went wrong. Her mother had no power. Still, Ericka had high regards for her father, as he raised her to be super-independent, which she was by now. She didn't realise that the same over-independence kept the kind of man she would have liked to meet at bay.

Attempting to fill the gap, she over-ate to reward herself when she achieved something, and to compensate for the lack of self-esteem, the lack of love, the lack of connectedness with herself.

Things shifted rapidly for Ericka, because she was absolutely ready to take a leap and to do what it takes to make sure she created different results. She found it easy to write a long list of triggers, with anger at the top of it, and began tuning in to her own B.B.C. anytime it showed up throughout each day, which was very often.

When I took her through the reconnection

between her conscious and subconscious mind, she experienced a healing, and felt a real connection with herself for the first time in her life. She lost 6 kilos within the next 12 weeks, without trying, and kept on losing weight steadily, which she never put back on. She worked on clearing her own programmes, and also opted for some direct clearing with me to speed up the process.

She joined dance classes, as we decided that joining a sitting-down meditation class would only reinforce her already prevalent 'masculine side' and type of activities in the office. She made some new friends, on par with her current energy levels, and even forgot about drinking wine during the week.

When she got more familiar with regular practise, she included her B.B.M.E. step while waiting at the coffee machine, while driving home from work, or waiting for her computer to load, all of which used to irritate her. She now feels she can handle any type of adversity, as she can use any of them to practise her steps. Whenever old anger came up, she addressed her subconscious mind and mentally said, 'I release you from anger'. She found that each time she did it, she got closer to her Inner Being, and actually began to fall in love with herself. A complete breakthrough for Ericka. She began to be drawn to drama classes and other activities that she would have never considered previously, or would have had the patience to attend or the courage to stand before others. She got near immediate results because she really used every occasion to free herself, and regain her natural resilience. Having freed her own mental space from constant worry, she began to study different ways that she could invest some of her money and take care of her own future. It was during an evening course on property investment that she met David. The rest is history as they say. All these shifts in her life began with one decision, the decision to help herself, and be committed enough to do what it takes to change her life.

Q&A

Q: Isn't clearing an emotion avoidance or denial?

A: Whenever an emotion comes up, and as you practise reconnecting with your Inner Being as often as possible, through your B.B.C. or your B.B.M.E., you will be able to determine if this is an ongoing, repetitive emotional condition, or a useful message to be acted upon in the moment. I feel that you already know the answer to that right now. Hurt happens, but suffering is optional.

In both of these scenarios, using your B.B.M.E. will help you not to drown in the emotions you feel. As mentioned earlier, it can be very appropriate to pause and note what message your emotions are delivering to you. Beyond this, acknowledge the emotion and the message, be grateful for it, and if there is something to be addressed, take the appropriate course of action.

The emotional clearing that takes place with

NeuroBiology Reprogramming™ is aimed to free you from the repetitive-type emotions that entrap you at every occasion. These are what I call your default setting(s), the emotional 'loop' that keeps you recreating the same occasion, so you get to feel the same feelings. As always, this works from the inside out. Until you get to these, you are holding yourself prisoner in a self-perpetuating loop.

Don't forget that the emotions are an expression of your subconscious thoughts, which is why it can be hard to recall what created it consciously, due to their unconscious nature. This is why your emotions are a fantastic pointer or cue to begin releasing what does not serve you. The beautiful thing is that you don't really need to know what the original thought is or when it began, the clearing will certainly take place. All you have to do is to be willing to let go.

In the example above, Ericka first came to me because of her anger. It didn't matter much what happened around her, her anger rose at the smallest occasion, including when she heard something that had nothing to do with her, like in the case of her friend's husband having an affair. For Ericka, any and every occasion was a cause for her emotional 'default setting' to literally erupt, causing havoc in her body and in her life.

She got quick results because she was absolutely sick of her life as it stood, and she was willing to use that same anger as her cue to practice her B.B.C. and B.B.M.E. She also began using the same anger to release her subconscious from the layers of rage that burdened her mind. There were many other programmes right behind the anger she felt, and all of them got deleted as she took care of the one that stood at the forefront, the one she could perceive.

NeuroBiology Reprogramming™ is not a therapy but a self-realisation practice. It allows you to get free, and not simply better, as is often the case with therapies.[21] We do not need to dwell on any past event, or put anyone through trauma again by revisiting a past memory. Instead, we simply use the present recurring emotions as a cue and a direction to use N.B.R. This is why Ericka got near immediate results. How wonderful!

Q: What about the positive emotions, do they need to be cleared?

A: Positive emotions are the fuel to creating great results, so you don't need to clear them, but you can certainly harness them. The most important relationship you can ever have is the one you have with yourself, so using your B.B.C. when you feel any of them, and anchoring them with a breath and your physical gesture allows you to program your own neurobiology with plenty of goodness and positivity. These positive states will then be easily recalled with a single breath or by using your physical gesture, which can be handy on a day when you don't feel so good or

---

[21] A handful of therapies can actually create breakthrough freedom.

so confident. This is the basis of resilience.

A small word of caution, however, which is that, expecting certain emotions to always be there, or to remain at the same level of intensity, creates expectations. Expectation is just another programme, responsible for a lot of pain, that usually leads to another, called disappointment. It also takes away from what contribution you might otherwise be able to make to a relationship, for example, to make sure that you express appreciation or do what it takes to maintain passion.

Let's say that you were deeply in love with your partner when you first met, and that you expected the feeling to always remain the same, although you didn't do anything to keep on nurturing the relationship. I don't have to tell you that this is obviously setting yourself up for a fall. The most powerful thing you could do in that situation would be to clear your own expectations ('I release you from . . .') so you can keep on moving in the direction of love, of communication, of appreciation, behaving in a way that is contributing to the love you want to receive. In short: always go first! While you can't control the outcome, you will have the best chances by contributing that which you want to receive.

One more thing, whatever kind of emotions are going on in you, remember that they are an attribute, and not who you are at the core. Emotions are just like clouds passing in the sky, or the range of sounds that can be produced by piano keys. Different thoughts will produce different emotions. They vary in intensity and are forever changeable. There are no right or wrong emotions. All that matters is that *you choose* how you want your life to be. You now have the understanding of your own internal and external mechanism of creation. You can steer your life in a direction that you want to experience.

Q: Isn't clearing an emotion inviting unscrupulous people to delete feelings that may otherwise allow them to ponder on a mistake they are just about to make?

A: Any questions are always best asked regarding ourselves, as we have no control over what someone else chooses to do. To find the answer to this, we can use the same two markers as I mentioned earlier on, as an answer to a similar question in the mental resilience chapter. In addition, and since we are exploring emotions here, we can 'check in' to note what kind of feelings arise in us following these two self-inquiries:

1. Is the decision I am about to make allowing others to benefit in some way, or is it purely self-serving?
2. Upon the application of that same decision, will I be leaving a profit or a deficit?

We can apply this to any financial, structural, physical, or emotional queries. If the answer is 'no' to one or both of these self-inquiries, I would review the decision and keep using your NeuroBiology Programming™ steps until the idea you have can produce positive outcomes all around, and therefore beneficial emotions.

Q: What if I keep feeling the same emotion but have no idea what belief it comes from? Can I trust that it will be cleared if I use my tools?

A: This will be the case for most repeating, emotional, 'default setting' type emotions. Because of the law of cause and effect, this particular emotion is echoing from a very long time ago. You probably registered it as a learned, unconscious habit that may have been in your family, and this could have started many generations back. It usually does, this is how family lineage is passed on. For example, this is certainly how alcoholism or abuse is perpetrated.

Let me ask you this: do you have trust in the Natural Intelligence that is organising your heart's beats right now, even if you don't believe in it? Can you count on it? Yes? Good. You can. Just in the same way, if you are willing to use your DELETE key whenever this particular emotion comes up, the job will be done. The conscious mind and the decision to let go by using the tools are the only defining factors for success.

I have seen it time and again.

This seems like a simple choice, yet often difficult to make as the resistance in us can be bigger than the desire to free ourselves. In this case, DELETE the resistance first. Then get to the emotion you are talking about.

I can tell from your question that you have not begun to use the steps. So right now, this translates as you asking from your fully 'programmed self'. When you begin to help yourself and use your tools, these questions will disappear. New ones may come from the practice, but for now, I invite you to begin your practice, and then simply get busy creating your new life.

Q: How long is it right to grieve the loss of a loved one?

A: You can grieve as long as you want, so long as your grief does not drown you or suppress your ability to be here for others, who equally deserve your love and attention. Most emotions have huge momentum, and grief is such an emotion. While it is normal to grieve for some time, if your emotions are swallowing up all your time and energy, be conscious that you are allowing it to do so.

The B.B.M.E. practice is essential during such times, as it can allow you to get a break from the grief, and save you from being engulfed by it. You could even choose an amount of time you think is fair to fully indulge in it.

Following this, and when you will feel that the time has come to rescue yourself, make a decision to increase tuning in to your B.B.M.E. to begin releasing yourself from the grief.

When you feel ready, you can change the

emotional signal from the thought of loss, which materialises as 'grief', to 'love'. Of course, you will still miss the departed person, but every time you think of them, if you choose to feel love over grief, you will find that the nature of your relationship will evolve, as you will always be connected in love. When we grieve, we focus on ourselves and the deficit we feel. When we focus on love, we are sharing our heart, which is an abundant and generous feeling that can benefit you, the departed, and all the people around you.

Q: Why are we not just focusing on the good feelings here, or using daily positive affirmations to be permanently happy?

A: Did you ever have a bout of several hard days, feeling really sad or downright depressed. Now imagine someone recommending that you 'just be happy', would you have wanted to smack them across the forehead? Jokes aside, when you look at the emotional scale, jumping right across the spectrum from sadness to happiness is far too much to ask of anyone, and, to be honest, quite unrealistic.

However, you can certainly get back to instant peace, and feel a measure of contentment, which you will get when using your tools. Who knows, happiness may arise after that! Do make sure that your happiness does not rely on anything external, or you are in big trouble. This would be 'conditional happiness', with the potential to disappear the minute the object of your happiness is no longer with you. Anything you want to experience is more real and more stable if it is 'an inside job' first.

Q: I use the law of attraction, is that not enough? Why bother using clearing tools at all?

A: I can think of three good reasons.

The first is that, while it is possible to override some things with sheer willpower, because you are indeed, very powerful, it is also highly probable that you may find out that you are not at all wired to handle, or to keep, what you received. A simple example of this is winning the lotto, only to lose all the money shortly, and often end up with a larger debt than was there before the big win. Or getting promoted to a leading position that we are not able to sustain, or fame that we cannot handle, etc. All of these are very common occurrences, and they may have started with daily positive affirmations.

The second is that positive affirmations have no answers when one gets diagnosed with a serious illness like cancer, for example. As you know, I speak from experience. We are all heavily programmed, and if something you want is not in your life at present, you will get to experience it quicker if you simply DELETE what is in the way of it. After that, using positive affirmations will work wonders, and you will be able to sustain what you received. Until then, asking for something we are not wired to be able to receive or utilise can in fact be very self-depreciating. This can be seriously counterproductive as most of us already carry an amount of self-disapproving programmes.

The third is, for real, long-lasting change that includes steady progress and success, your own internal wiring has to be congruent with itself. This means that your mind—your ultimate creating tool—must function in unison with itself, and not against itself as we studied in the chapter on mental resilience. Unless they are using some similar tools and processes, the mind of most people you know is literally 'fragmented', meaning that the conscious mind emits 'positive thinking' while the subconscious runs the only programmes it can: what is there and has always been there, until cleared out. It cannot do anything else, as this is your biological computer, running according to the information that is recorded in it. This is why overriding a program doesn't work anywhere near as well as clearing it.

If you are wanting something you cannot get, there is a program that is creating the lack. Clear this, and you can easily get to it, guaranteed. This is more about precise neuroscience than wishful thinking. EEGs can show what kind of waves the brain emits and, with it, the different hormones that are produced. Different feelings engage different actions, which means that we get different results. This means that your body reacts accordingly to the thought-forms it receives, and at 20 million bits per second coming from the subconscious, versus 14 bits from the conscious . . . this is obviously a losing battle. At least until the mind is fully congruent with itself. [Stay tuned for Physical Resilience, coming up in the next chapter.]

As we studied extensively, when the mind is not connected, it works against itself. We consciously ask for something, but our own subconscious programming says otherwise. We are all familiar with setting out to do something we really want, like write ourselves a 1.000.000 euro check, only to hear the voice in the head that says, 'No way, that's not possible for you'. This is exactly what depletes our resilience 'reservoir'. No matter how much or how often we repeat a positive statement, it does not prepare us to handle what we are asking for. As we keep on asking, and not getting the results intended, our resilience dwindles, understandably.

We remain like the character in Tolstoy's story, begging for what is already ours, while living an entire life of poverty, yet sitting on a casket of gold, not realising that the treasure is already within us.

Sometimes the lesson for us is to get what we want, just so that we can see that we have to build internal resources to develop it and keep it. This is why many millionaires lose all their money several times, until they learn to keep it. You can apply this concept to anything you want, such as a relationship, a particular role or position, taking your business to the next level, etc.

When you have the wherewithal to diligently clear the obstacles that naturally come up as you unpack and deploy your human potential, you can keep taking steady new steps forward, and build something that will last and have all the success you intended ... and more! Once you can do that, you can certainly bring back daily affirmations.

In fact, we will do even better than that, and use an incredible tool to maximise the power of your mind in The Master Plan, in the last chapter.

LET'S TALK STORY!

The Gates of Paradise

A soldier named Nobushige came to Hakuin and asked: 'Is there really a paradise and a hell?'

'Who are you?' inquired Hakuin.

'I am a samurai,' the warrior replied.

'You, a soldier!' exclaimed Hakuin. 'What kind of ruler would have you as his guard? Your face looks like that of a beggar.'

Nobushige became so angry that he began to draw his sword, but Hakuin continued: 'So you have a sword! Your weapon is probably much too dull to cut off my head.'

As Nobushige drew his sword, Hakuin remarked: 'Here open the gates of hell!'

At these words, the samurai, perceiving the master's discipline, sheathed his sword and bowed.

'Here open the gates of paradise,' said Hakuin.

CHAPTER 7—PRACTICE RECAP

N.B.R. LEVEL TWO: EMOTIONAL RESILIENCE

Daily practice

- Pranayama breathing morning and night. Maximum time investment 3 minutes twice a day.

'On the go' practice

- Apply your DELETE key (your favourite colour) to any recurring, limiting emotion, or mentally say, think or see the phrase 'I release you from . . .'

- Take a breath, and use your physical gesture to anchor your new state in your neurobiology.

Once you have done that TAKE A STEP in the direction of your desired outcome.

CHAPTER 8

NEUROBIOLOGY REPROGRAMMING™

LEVEL THREE: PHYSICAL RESILIENCE

"Self-discipline is a form of freedom. Freedom from laziness and lethargy, freedom from the expectations and demands of others, freedom from weakness and fear—and doubt. Self-discipline allows a pitcher to feel his individuality, his inner strength, his talent. He is master of, rather than a slave to, his thoughts and emotions."

— H.A. Dorfman

Last but far from least, as we conclude our plan to optimal, bulletproof resilience, we look at the physical body and how you can gain mastery over it.

WHAT IS THE PHYSICAL BODY?

The physical body—its state of health, energy and well-being—is the product of our thoughts and emotions combined. It is the result and not the cause of our feelings. This effectively means that our body is NOT an immovable structure, but rather a condensed expression of all programmes, including thoughts, feelings, decisions, actions, and the environment in which we immerse ourselves.

Knowing what you do by now, this ought to be a mind shift, and possibly a breakthrough. It means that, when you clear an old subconscious programme, new emotions are made available to you, creating new feelings, and therefore new beliefs. These beliefs literally change your physical state, which helps you to make different decisions and take different steps. This is precisely when your external reality cannot help but match your internal creative process. This sums up your Master-Creator abilities. You can literally bend reality: this means that you are the ONE![22] The following diagram contains the last addition of the uses and

---

[22] Reference to *The Matrix* movie—also known as a documentary!

functions of the physical body, which makes the internal mechanism of creation complete, as depicted by the downward arrows.

YOU
The Complete Internal Mechanism of Creation

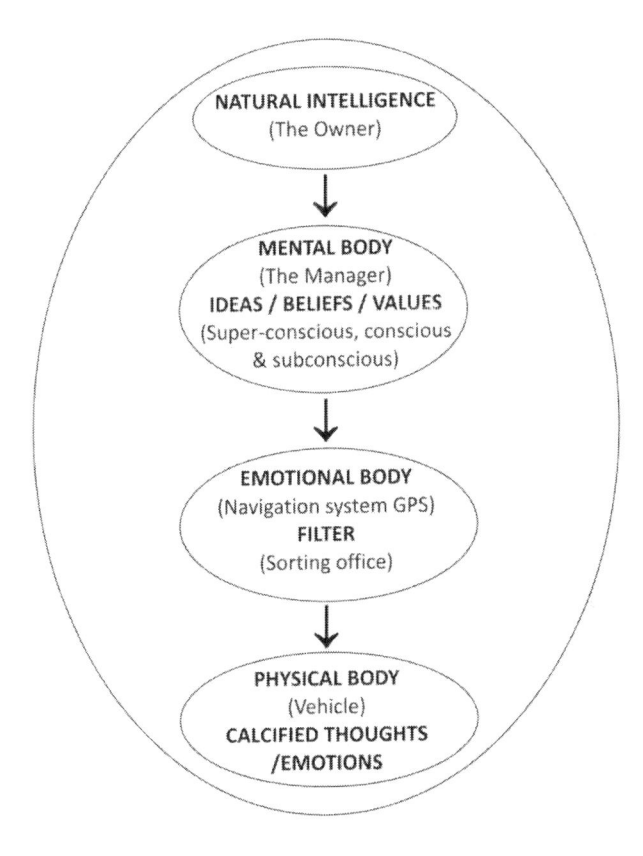

NATURAL INTELLIGENCE
(The Owner)

↓

MENTAL BODY
(The Manager)
IDEAS / BELIEFS / VALUES
(Super-conscious, conscious & subconscious)

↓

EMOTIONAL BODY
(Navigation system GPS)
FILTER
(Sorting office)

↓

PHYSICAL BODY
(Vehicle)
CALCIFIED THOUGHTS /EMOTIONS

This diagram outlines the famous declaration: *"All men were created equal"*. I would add that, once we have the necessary information, as we now do, it is then up to us, according to our own creative power, to make use of THAT which was given to us: the amazing potential that is within each of us, awaiting our participation.

Taking a Personal Inventory

As we take a moment to look all around us, and take stock of what is going on in our own life, we can see how we have contributed to our state of health and energy, our posture, our attitude, our marriage, our family, our bank account, our business, our investments, our sense of purpose and contribution, our level of passion and zest for life, our relationships with people, the situation at hand, etc. This is why I renamed the physical body 'calcified thoughts and emotions'. While it may be 'calcified' enough for us to take stock of it, to unmistakably see the results, it can also be changed. It is like an indicator that allows us to see the sum total of our thoughts and feelings, and gives us the impetus to initiate the changes we need to make so we can experience the new. This is only possible if we know it is possible.

Although it may be difficult and even painful to take such an inventory in some cases, this insight affords us the capacity to take responsibility. It give us the fuel, the resilience we need to make the changes necessary. Taking a personal inventory may feel daunting at first, especially if we are used to blaming external circumstances for our present dealings or situation. However, taking responsibility is a gift, as it actually means that we are taking our power back, or harnessing it, and carving a new destiny for ourselves.

Either we like what we see, choose to do more of the same and even 'turn up the volume' to improve upon it, or it is time to make some changes. Making effective changes means clearing our mindset and making new decisions, as this is at the top of our internal creating capacity.

MY EXPERIENCE WITH CANCER

I have had first-hand experience with the results of this mechanism with many things in my life, many of which were wonderfully positive. I went from being as close to the poverty line as anyone one can be without being homeless. I went from being very broke to financially independent and secure, heading toward financial freedom. Today, I am living in the house of my dreams, travelling the world, contributing to people in a meaningful way, constantly learning new skills, doing what I love most. I jump out of bed every morning and cannot wait to unpack the day! I can safely say that I would never be where I am today, feeling the way I do, without the daily and thorough use of my own tools, and the ability to clear my mindset, which was loaded with many limiting beliefs. While this is still a work in progress, it is something that has become as familiar and as easy as taking a shower.

Slightly harder and far more serious, I got a chance to test the same method I am sharing with you here—NeuroBiology Reprogramming™—when I was diagnosed with cancer in 2010. The steps I used are precisely what I am sharing with you in this book, which is why I am 100% confident that this works. Although I do not recommend anyone do the same, but rather follow their own guidance, I chose not to avail of any treatment of any kind, allopathic or natural medicine. This was not at all a heroic or irresponsible decision, but rather an intelligent choice based on what I firmly understand, and teach. My own sense of integrity allowed me to decide that, if this didn't work for me, I would no longer teach this method, since it clearly did not work. So when I was given the diagnosis, I simply chose to hear it as an indicator rather than a declining state of health over which I had no control.

Although I must say that I was not consciously aware of fearing cancer in the least, I did spend four years in a terrible neighbourhood being bullied, which caused me to feel extreme fear and worry on a daily basis. While it would have been tempting to attribute the daily fear I felt to cancer, I also accepted the fact that this whole situation may have been the result and not the cause of what was happening. The law of cause and effect presides over all lifetimes, and is far reaching. This means that we come in carrying many—subconscious—beliefs of which we are completely unaware. As I said before, the origin of any problem doesn't matter as much as doing what it takes in the moment and simply clearing it.

When I heard the diagnosis, I did not take it to be a permanent state of health, moving in the direction of inevitable decline. I realised that I had a choice. I chose to believe that by nature, I am wellness, I am life force, I am resilience. This left me with only having to clear any thoughts-forms that spoke against these simple truths, such as 'doubt', 'fear', or 'asking for healing', etc. Physiologically speaking, this effectively meant that my body experienced a state of trust instead of fear, which is to say, a state of alkaline instead of acid. Alkaline is the environment in which the body can be in best health, and acid is the breeding ground of ill-health. While I chose trust over fear, deep love and appreciation of self rather than anything else, the Natural Intelligence that is the origin of us all got to do its job, uninterrupted by fear-based thoughts or beliefs.

I also took immediate action, which was to look for a house, even though my financial and structural situation meant that this was near impossible. Yet, one thing led to another, I moved my children and myself to a safe and regular neighbourhood, and got to experience spontaneous remission.

We Feel What We Think and Think What We Feel

It is, of course, more challenging to change something once it has already physically manifested, because of the feeling that it engages. When we hear difficult news, we feel what we think almost immediately, and unless we become mindful and choose to delete the fear-based thoughts, we end up thinking what we feel. This means that we can literally get locked in a self-perpetuating loop. This is putting ourselves through unnecessary hardship, especially when we need all the resilience we can get to turn our health or our business around, improve a relationship, or anything else that has to change.

NATURE OF THE PHYSICAL BODY

In order to really appreciate how awesome our physical body really is, we can benefit from studying it dispassionately. While looking at it in this way is valid for men and women, it may be more pertinent for the women reading this. This is because women are loaded with programming that is based in disapproving of their own body-image. Programmes such as 'comparison' are rife, reinforced by the mass media, which still portrays unrealistic or airbrushed pictures of what beauty is supposed to look like.

Therefore, looking at the human body in scientific terms can facilitate the realisation of its awesome power and capacity, its intricate mechanism and infinite beauty. Simply learning about its potential can literally increase your resilience level the moment you read about it. This is because neurotransmitters and relevant hormones are fired into action according to the thoughts and emotions you entertain in each moment. This, like the rest of your human potential, is far beyond what you have been led to believe until now. Choose carefully what you are reading and watching, as you are literally 'breathing it in' your neurobiology.

The physical body is:

- A vibrational translator of the world around us via our five senses: taste, smell, sight, touch, and hearing.
- Our vehicle and temple.
- The container with which we can experience what we create, through our own individuality.
- A tangible expression, or the reflection, of our thoughts and emotions—our beliefs.

Our body is not a structure but a process
of the information we hold in our mind
and the emotions we feel.
Its state of health and energy can change
as we choose different conscious thoughts,
and clear the beliefs that do not serve us.

Please take the opportunity to use your B.B.C. as you read the words above. Take a deep breath and, with it, the opportunity to use your physical gesture to anchor it. This is how words can resonate past the intellectual mind, straight into your subconscious mind. You can read it several times. This is how you create new habits. This is also when intellectual knowledge can be transmuted into wisdom.

Harnessing Body Intelligence

Between our skin, red blood cells, organs, and tissues, cell renewal takes place every few days, over several weeks and months, and even up to several years. This means that most of our body gets a chance to start anew in terms of health and potential. This also means that we can literally think and feel our way to wellness. You are a Master-Creator and, from today onward, you have each and every tool to begin living on purpose rather than by default. You are the Architect of your own life and can redesign what you want to improve upon in every way. This is an amazing capacity, enjoy it!

THE NATURE OF WORLDLY SUCCESS

We see the world according to our own beliefs and values, which is to say our own conscious and subconscious thoughts, and our own emotions.

> *"We don't see things as they are,
> we see them as we are."* — Anaïs Nin

This means that the world we see is the projected map through which we can recognise our own internal landscape. As Dr. Bruce Lipton describes it, our life is basically "a printout of our subconscious mind". We are all excellent at believing that what we see that displeases us has nothing to do with us. I will be totally honest with you and say that, although extremely brief, this is still my initial response—until I remember to use my own tools!

As you use this incredibly precise mechanism, you can begin to correct the mindset that is creating the hardship in your life, or equally fine-tune it to increase the success you have in mind. Until then, it is just like wearing belief-tinted glasses, as your perceptions colour all your experiences, and as a consequence, the results you experience.

Try this simple experiment:

- Take a look around the room where you are sitting right now.
- Set a timer and take note of how many yellow objects you can see in 30 seconds.
- When the timer rings, close your eyes, and keep your eyes closed.
- Now, can you recall how many blue objects you saw around the room?

You are going to say, 'But, Mahayana, you said yellow, not blue! I have no idea how many blue objects are there!' I say that you are 100% accurate. We can only see what our mind is seeking to recognise . . . and miss everything else that is there. This is precisely why doing something new with an old mindset is not possible. The mind cannot detect the solution until we upgrade our own 'mental software' to actually recognise something that may have been there all along. Or perhaps to be opened to learning something new.

Research in neuroscience shows that, unless trained to broaden, the mind keeps replicating the same patterns. When we encounter something difficult, we look to get an answer from someone else, rather than seek to get our own answers. Now, think about that for a second . . . Even if the person you are asking has the greatest of experience, it is also true that they can only answer according to their own programming. So choose carefully who you lean on, if you do, and be aware of their limitations. We all have them.

Looking for an answer to a solution outside ourselves, rather than trusting our own knowing happens for two main reasons.

The first is that we have been trained 'what to think' rather than 'how to think'. This many have been the way it was in your household, and, of course, it was certainly the way we were all taught in school.

The second is that, since we were young, we have been trained to give our power away to teachers, doctors, priests, etc. This is why re-establishing internal trust, including listening to your own intuition or gut feeling, can be challenging. Yet, these are the best 'internal compasses' to know what direction to follow, and how to take each new step forward. Of course, even when you are comfortable with using your own intuition, and/or listening to your own inspiration, it will undoubtedly involve other people, or learning something new, as 'no man or woman is an island!'

> *"Each of us need all of us,*
> *and all of us need each of us."* — Jim Rohn

Making New Friends on Your Way to Success

In order to lead yourself out of a challenging situation—particularly if it is a familiar, recurring one—or to take yourself to the next level, the success created will depend on your mindset, first and foremost. The only thing that can hold you back is F.E.A.R. (False Event Appearing Real), which will include all your personal mindset limitations.

At such a time, do choose very carefully who you talk to and with whom you share your dreams and decisions. You need support, and not fear-based comments that will make you hesitant or fearful. Remember, each can only speak according to their own programming, according to their own experience. If someone you loved and trusted so far, now appears to pull you down when you express new, far-reaching goals and decisions, it is only because of their own limitations. Don't take it personally. They can only see it the way they see it.

Instead, choose people that have already accomplished what you want to do or be. This could mean that, while you take a leap to the next level, you are leaving some friends or colleagues behind. The real ones, the ones that support you no matter what, will stay. Some will leave and new ones will arrive. It's all good!

As you choose to use the tools given here, unprecedented opportunities, solutions and results will be created. Guaranteed.

Q&A

Q: I believe that changing my physical state can change how I feel, which can also help me to change my mind, what do you say about this?

A: I say that you are absolutely right. You can do it that way too; whether you focus on affecting the physical body first or last, you will benefit, at least for some things. This is precisely why I recommended that you anchor each new routine you learnt throughout the book with a chosen physical gesture. This defines and sums up the practice of NeuroBiology Reprogramming™, as you are literally training your nervous system with a new kind of wiring.

However, because the subconscious mind governs each feeling, which is to say influences what we can produce in terms of results, it doesn't always work. While it may be easy for some things to be transformed solely with willpower, which is effectively using the power of the conscious mind alone, it will always remain limited because of what we know about the power of the subconscious mind, and its momentum.

My favourite choice and course of action for you would be to have both parts of your mind working in synchronicity, be able to clear any obstacle as they rise, and use your willpower to take new steps forward, to make sure that you are using your full capacity. A more precise and powerful use of both attributes. This is when you become unstoppable.

Q: If I only want to become physically resilient, do I still have to prioritise changing my mindset?

A: Physical resilience comes from mental resilience, with the in-between determining factor being the emotions. This is how you can develop unshakable beliefs. Olympic athletes are trained to develop ultimate resilience by envisioning themselves winning, by using mental conditioning. Research shows that when an athlete visualises running, for example, their neuromuscular activity registers the movement as if he or she were really physically running. The body doesn't know if what goes though the mind is real or not, but will react as a response of the thoughts being emitted, both conscious and unconscious. Such is your awesome mind-power!

So while you may choose to use sheer physical determination, which is similar to the question answered before this one, your physical state of health and energy will become far more resilient if you include changing your mindset as you do. For optimal progress, results and success, I highly recommend you use your three attributes. Leaving a part of you out is cutting yourself short of your true potential.

Q: I have felt as though my spirit was broken when I lost my job, and then failed again as I set up a company that did not work out. Where can I start?

A: It is not possible to break the human spirit of someone who is connected to their own source. Think of Braveheart, screaming 'Freedom!' as the guillotine comes down. Whether you actually believe that you are connected to Source or not, the truth is that you are. You wouldn't be taking the next breath if that weren't true. This means that resilience is yours by nature. You are resilience. I can tell you right now that the success you seek is much closer than you think. The only thing that has been adding layers over this innate resilience are your own beliefs, made from thoughts you adopted as your own, powered up by emotions, which is why they had momentum. Today, this is finished. DELETE those beliefs, and you have exactly what it takes to make it happen, as beliefs are the stifling layers that sit over your natural resilience, already there. Blow these out, and you win. Guaranteed.

Let me tell you something you already know: life can be hard at times, but you are not without power to resolve what comes your way. In fact, we can accurately say that challenges present themselves to give you the opportunity to access the stuff that is available to you: your untapped potential. Of course, by conscious choice, you or I would obviously never choose to put ourselves though these kind of challenges. Yet these represent the in-between circumstantial elements that help you build the bridge between where you are and where you want to go. Be grateful for it. Life is a journey and not a destination.

First, your mindset has to undergo a transformation. Make a decision, and DELETE all the programs that are in your way, and as they come up moment by moment. Every time you feel a little trust in yourself, a little relief, a little peace, take a conscious breath and anchor this state with your chosen physical gesture.

Second, develop self-discipline, including the steps you learnt here. Do your pranayama breathing twice a day, and use every occasion to reconnect with your core power, your Inner Being. You deserve the investment. You can do that through your B.B.C. and your B.B.M.E.

Thirdly, keep taking steps in the direction of your goals, while using all the above so you keep carving new tracks. See and feel yourself as a 'PATH FINDER'. When you see / think / feel the word 'failure' in your mind, know that it means 'ONE STEP CLOSER TO MY GOAL'. Repeat this 3 times, take a breath, and anchor it. These are tools tailor-made, just for you, to help you forge forward.

You can do this; you have the energy and the

knowledge of the Creator inside you. You are the incarnation of the Creator in human form, in your present body. Breathe this in, anchor it.

Don't forget to make a huge deal of every success, no matter how seemingly small. Any good news is worth celebrating.

Lastly, and if need be for a while, the truth is that you could live on a bowl of rice a day, in a tiny room, while you rebuild your life. You would still have access to the most precious and powerful resources any king may have, the essence of true sovereignty: your mind and its creative capacity when connected to Source, Natural Intelligence. This is true wealth, the kind that cannot be taken away, regardless of your physical and structural location or condition.

My guess is that, if you are here, now, you have what it takes to turn this around. As you begin to use the tools given here and the personal tools I just gave you, you will begin to feel your self-confidence and your self-esteem rise again. When you feel your own power rise, trust me, you will find the experience to be as cumulative as any past failure. You will experience rapid and positive momentum as soon as you turn your own 'mind switch' on and begin to commit to yourself and to your own potential.

The only question is: are you ready? Yes? Good.

Q (from CEO): If I am willing to clear my own beliefs and perceptions, does it mean that everyone in the company will be happy and doing their best. Can I

expect the culture to be transformed?

A: Expectations and the desire for external control are programs that are best if cleared out. Everyone has free will. Everyone creates particular results, according to their own mindset, or internal wiring. Most people create by default, because they don't know the rules of the game or how to win it, meaning that they don't know who they are or how they function. They are living by default and not on purpose.

There are two things to bear in mind here. The first is that you cannot control your environment, at least not without exhausting yourself, creating limited results and plenty of frustration. However, you can certainly contribute to it by inspiring people to take action, as you cultivate a vision that includes the people around you, and communicate about it effectively. We will look at leadership skills shortly, and in particular at communication.

Second, the work discussed in this book is very much about making use of one's own personal capacity and increased potential. While it would be most beneficial, of course, that everyone in the company has access to these materials, much can be accomplished by individuals such as yourself, taking responsibility to make the necessary internal shifts. I guarantee you that you will find it to be an extraordinary thing, that when you are willing to change a particular belief you hold, and without doing much else, you will see external shifts and changes happening all around you. Most of them with little to no interference on your part. This is because we create not from the outside in, but the inside out.

Q: In order to attain an amount of self-mastery over my physical body, what kind of food do you recommend?

A: This may sound controversial, but food is the last nutrient that your body needs, unless you are a developing child or a young adult. The ultimate and simplest health regime, in order of importance, is as follows:

1. Air
2. Water
3. Food

Air, or 'breath', is what you need to take in the most, particularly through the practices included, if you seek self-mastery. This is wonderful, and I highly recommend everyone does this.

We have studied about breath being our most primal and essential nutrient, since you cannot go without it for more than a few minutes. It is also the carrier of information for the cells in your body, all 50-70 trillions of them, and very much influences your health potential, based on whether enough of it can get all the way down your lungs. Shallow breathing as a habit, or typical of someone who is experiencing anxiety, and means that a portion of the oxygen inside the lungs is never replenished. Being able to take in more oxygen, while feeling gratitude or any other empowering thoughts and feelings, can contribute tremendously to accessing your mental, and therefore physical, resilience.

Water is the body's next essential nutrient. Although the intake required varies based on many different factors such as age, gender, weight, activities, etc. and what part of the body we are talking about (brain, cells, organs, etc.) it can average 60-75% of our total body mass. This makes water pretty important. More often than not, and especially if one is weight-conscious, it is easy to think we may be hungry, when in fact, we are thirsty.[23]

If you don't actually feel thirsty—but feel like snacking often—and/or haven't developed the discipline to drink water, count it a priority. Don't wait to feel thirsty as this is a wiring that your body is not familiar with, a habit you haven't yet developed.

Aside from the fact that many degenerative illnesses are linked to a lack of it, water is also a powerful regenerator. It allows the lymphatic system to flush toxins out, and keeps your largest excretory organ—your skin—in its best condition. When you use your clearing tools, and beyond your mental and emotional bodies being cleared from beliefs, the last place where programmes are held is in physical tissues.

---

[23] See my book Mahayana's Rejuvenating Manual, written for men and women who want to maximize their physical potential, age gracefully and in good health.

So drinking water and eating water-rich foods are essential.

Food is the last nutrient you need, contrary to popular belief. The body has done what it needs in terms of growth by the time we reach 21-25 years old. In general, and unless we practise a lot of physical activities that demand we consume more 'fuel', we eat much more food than we need to. Very basically, food is meant as medicine to the body. If you will just bear that in mind, it will naturally steer you in the direction of what your body needs exactly. Inner guidance is the perfect thing to select what really would work best for you, as there are so many schools of thought on the subject, that it can be hard to know what is best. Your body knows, so listen to it. However, here are some thoughts and guidelines to help you.

Many people use food as comfort, reward or as a numbing mechanism, which is anything but what food is meant to be. While there is absolutely no problem with occasional indulgence, the 80/20 Pareto principle also works very well here to make sure that we eat healthy food 80% of the time, and can indulge 20% of the time. This is a general guideline that is not too strict or too loose.

Added to this, and unless you are reasonably health conscious, most of us eat acid-forming food on a constant basis, with a far too little alkaline-forming food intake.[24] This is the root cause of many illnesses, as it goes hand in hand with acid-forming thoughts: the fear-based ones like stress, worry, guilt, self-hatred, etc. Your state of physical health largely depends on whether your body is acidic most of the time, or alkaline. As mentioned earlier, acid is the breeding ground for illness, and alkaline is the ground for good health. While you may be 100% health conscious, and eat the very best foods, homemade and organic, you may still fall short of the anticipated results of best health and vibrancy, depending on your inner dialogue. This is because your mind influences how you process the food you ingest. In short, and beyond choosing what you feel is best for you, DELETE any self-depreciating thoughts if they come up before or while you eat.

If you are experiencing some strong emotions such as anger, for example, take a moment to use your B.B.M.E. and eat when you feel calmer. The last thing you need is an anger sandwich.

Q: How could my body be in an acidic or alkaline environment based on my thoughts alone?

A: Our bodies are mainly water, and, as you probably already know, water is a powerful conductor of energy. Aside from the fact that each of our cell's receptors captivates our thoughts and emotions,[25] and that our

---

[24] A full list can be found in my book Mahayana's Rejuvenating Manual.

[25] Check out the science of epigenetics, as described by Dr. Bruce

cells behave according to that information, it is carried around our organism via the water in your body. Have a look at Dr. Masaru Emoto's research to have a visual depiction of how the emotions we feel affect any water molecules, including the ones in our body.

So when we entertain thoughts based in self-hatred, guilt or worry, for example *trying to* NOT put on any extra weight while stuffing down a third donut, there is no way the body can even digest it properly. Equally, if we entertain enough stress or other disempowering emotions while we eat, we are not doing ourselves any favours. No matter how wonderfully healthy, organic or slimming the food we eat, we are ingesting what emotions we feel with every mouthful.

The same goes for cooking for the family while feeling preoccupied or angry, for example. Any emotions we feel go into the food we prepare. It is best to use the 3 steps given in this book while you cook, while making a cup of tea, or even handing over a glass of water to someone. A cup of tea made in worry or resentment never tastes as good as a cup of love, appreciation or gratitude.

Contrary to popular belief, mealtimes are not the best time to have a 'family talk', especially if it is likely to end up in confrontation. You can see why . . .

You may find the following controversial, but it is possible to ultimately transform the nature of the food

---

Lipton in his book *The Biology of Belief*.

you eat and how it affects you by your thoughts alone. This is called self-mastery, and a wonderful skill to develop, particularly handy to clear out allergies.

A client of mine, a lady who loved muffins, got over her gluten allergy by simply clearing the thought that said she was allergic. This one thought stood in front of many more self-depreciating programmes, but all these cleared within a few days as she used her tools. She is now as slim and beautiful as ever, and able to indulge once a day in a blueberry muffin. Guilt free!

Remember that your thoughts determine the outcome, always. Your perceptions define your experience.

RESILIENCE AND SELF-ESTEEM TOOLS

Beyond using the same process as for your mental and emotional processes, these three exercises will help restore your self-esteem. Self-esteem is about being able to love and appreciate every part of you, to know that you are enough, and loveable just as you are.

These exercises will unlock many other programmes that are linked to lack in your relationship, your self-confidence, your ability to create the success you want in your professional life, and your health and energy levels. Working with many different people in many different countries allowed me to see that most people suffer some version of this, so these exercises are good for everyone, even if the conscious mind says that there is enough self-esteem in you. A quick test for this is to note how long you can go with mentally criticising yourself.

You can read the following three tools anytime you feel the need to, or feel inspired to do so.

Tool 1—Love Your Body

For physical resilience, self-esteem, self-healing, self-appreciation, self-confidence, and to reconnect to your body.

'My body is my friend.
Thank you for being my vehicle, carrying me where I want to go, day after day, moment per moment.
I love you and respect you,
your shape, your abilities and limitations.
Please forgive me for having mistreated you, criticised you, compared you, and, at times, abused you, when all along you have, in fact, been my ally, vehicle and temple.
I love you, thank you.'

Tool 2—Heal Your Body

For physical resilience, self-healing, weight loss/gain, addictions, illnesses, allergies, and other blockages.

Read before eating food, especially if you

experience recurring thoughts based in self-disapproval, self-hatred or self-criticism.

> *'I completely trust my body's natural ability
> to self-regulate with the same Natural Intelligence
> that already orchestrates everything
> with absolute perfection.'*

Tool 3—Love Who You Are

To reconnect with the utmost source of well-being, abundance, resilience, and to improve any relationship with anyone in your personal and professional life.

Practise the following exercise twice a day until you absolutely love and appreciate who you are. I am not talking about vanity, self-inflation or narcissism, but rather about true appreciation of who you are. The relationship with yourself is the most important one you will ever have, as everything else in your life is an extension of it. No matter who comes and goes, your own relationship with yourself remains, so it might as well be a really good one!

If your mind is already putting up an argument why you can't do this, DELETE the belief that holds you up. Please know that the part of your face you will be focusing on is your eyes. This will make it easy, because as you do, you will recognise your own soul, and naturally be awed by its beauty.

DELETE whatever thought-forms come up in the

form of self-criticism; they are only programmes you took on board, waiting to be cleared.

Find a mirror. Look into your own eyes and say:

'(fill in your name), *I love you. You are enough just as you are. You are loveable just as you are. I love you entirely and completely. You deserve the very best that life has to offer.*'

CHAPTER 8—PRACTICE RECAP

N.B.R. LEVEL THREE: PHYSICAL RESILIENCE

RESILIENCE AND SELF-ESTEEM TOOLS FOR THE PHYSICAL BODY

TOOL 1—LOVE YOUR BODY

TOOL 2—HEAL YOUR BODY

TOOL 3—LOVE WHO YOU ARE

THE FULL PRACTICE RECAP

PART ONE

I.P.A. Integrated Practice Awareness

Tune in to your B.B.C.: Your Body Breath Connection. Connect with your breath, and feel your feet on the ground.

Tune in to your B.B.M.E.: Your Body Breath Mental Emotional practice to lean in to your core, your Inner Being, and to get respite from the mind-emotion grip.

A reminder for both practices is to use the list of things that annoy you or delight you as your cues.

To anchor both practices in your neurobiology chose a discreet physical gesture that you can practise right after you use your B.B.C. or your B.B.M.E. practice.

THE FULL PRACTICE RECAP

PART TWO

NeuroBiology Reprogramming™

Part One: One-time practice
- Name your subconscious and reconnecting statement

Part Two: Daily practice
- Pranayama breathing morning and night—energy refuel before your day starts or your night's sleep

Part Three: Moment per moment clearing practice
- Apply your DELETE key (in your own colour) or mentally say, 'I release you from . . .' to clear any limiting beliefs
- Take a regular breath to circulate this state throughout your whole body, and use your physical gesture to anchor it

Take ACTION—Take PHYSICAL STEPS to actualise the decisions you have made, so you can close the gap between where you are and what you want to experience.

The 3 steps together: B.B.C., B.B.M.E. and the clearing of beliefs sum up NeuroBiology Reprogramming™

PART THREE

THE MASTER PLAN

THE HEART OF LEADERSHIP

PARENTING SKILLS

REVERSE ENGINEERING

THE DOOR

"A captain of industry was looking for an able and wise manager who would have the skills and acuity to take over the running of the organisation after he had retired. He assembled the best managers from his own company and hired recruitment consultants and headhunters to find him additional ones who might serve his purpose.

On a particular day, all the possible contenders were assembled in a great hall of a mighty palace, which the organisation had hired for that day.

The captain of industry addressed the assembled handpicked managers. 'I have a problem, and I want to know who among you has the wherewithal to solve it. What you see in the wall behind me is the biggest, mightiest, and heaviest door in the kingdom. Who among you, without assistance, has the power to open it?'

Some of the managers simply shook their heads. It was just too big a problem. Others examined the door more closely, discussed aspects of leverage and mass, remembered theories of problem solving they had learned in business school, and admitted that it seemed to be an impossible task.

When the wisest and most respected had accepted defeat, all the others capitulated too.

Only one manager approached the door and gave it a thorough close up examination. He tapped it, assessed its width and depth, noticed the nature and

lubrication of its hinges. He checked it thoroughly with his eyes and hands. Prodding here, pushing there, poking there. Finally he made his decision. He breathed deeply, centred himself, and pulled gently on the door.

It swung open easily and effortlessly.

The others had made the assumption that the door had been locked or jammed. In fact it had been left ever so slightly ajar and the carpentry and design were so excellent only the slightest touch was required to open it.

The captain of industry had his successor, the leader he sought out. He addressed the managers assembled there. 'Success in life and industry depends on certain key things. They are these as we have seen demonstrated. First, rely on your senses to fully understand the reality of what is going on around you. Second, do not make false assumptions. Third, be willing to make tough decisions. Fourth, have the courage to act with boldness and conviction. Fifth, put your powers into action. Finally, do not be afraid to make mistakes.''

— *Oriental Source*

CHAPTER 9

THE HEART OF LEADERSHIP

"My will shall shape my future. Whether I fail or succeed shall be no man's doing but my own. I am the force; I can clear any obstacle before me or I can be lost in the maze. My choice; my responsibility; win or lose, only I hold the key to my destiny."

— Elaine Maxwell

As I proposed at the beginning of this book, whether you work in a leading capacity or not, I highly recommend that you see yourself as a leader from today onward. Even if you have no work at present, and are raising a family,[26] this will benefit you tenfold, as parenting is essentially leadership—leadership with a heart, the right kind of leadership. This is the most powerful and inspirational style of leadership. Thinking of yourself as a leader will help you to raise your standards all around, make you self-directed, which is an attractive quality for both men and women, perhaps even more so for a man. Becoming a leader will boost your resilience levels.

If you are an employee and want to get ahead, thinking of yourself as a leader is the fastest route to you getting promoted. In the words of Jim Rohn, *"If you want to attract more things in your life, you have to make yourself more attractive"*, meaning, of course, more valuable. Developing initiative, taking steps forward and seeing how and where you might be able to do more than your share are valuable qualities to develop. Learning new, relevant skills and above anything else, developing one's own personal resources, communication skills and cultivating desire to serve a cause beyond one's own needs are some of the hallmarks of leadership. At least the kind of leader

---

[26] This is one of the most important jobs in the world, as you are raising 'the future' of all of us. An honourable and highly challenging task, that will teach you more than any other position of power.

that is increasingly in demand in the organisation of today. Many companies prize attitude over skills, as any skills can be learned, but an attitude is usually there for good, or much harder to shift.

Consciousness-oriented organisations care for their employees. They see the value of providing personal development courses for everyone and coaching for executives. Some have areas on site where people can relax, and offer different schedules such as flexi-time instead of the 9-5 cycle, which have proven to be a great success in terms of job-fulfilment. Gratitude and appreciation toward employees, and celebration and group outings all contribute to an outstanding work culture.[27]

Leadership Qualities

Leaders and entrepreneurs have many good qualities. While there are many more than are listed below, here are some positive traits or characteristics that successful leaders and entrepreneurs have in common:

- Smart and fast—able to process a lot of information at high speed.

- Incredibly sharp memory.

---

[27] Check out Mindvalley, voted the 6-time winner of the World's Most Democratic Workplace Award.

- Able to deal with an amount of fear and keep taking calculated risks or decisions to move team/project forward.

- Delegating roles and duties.

- Have enough foresight and confidence to create scenarios based on innovation—to stay ahead of competition.

- Quick to analyse a situation and intellectually solve problems.

- Able to handle damage control and have enough calm and confidence to inspire a team to get back on their feet.

Having all these qualities can mean that it is hard to consider that we may need to learn some new skills, or change a particular style of leadership that may have propelled us to where we are today. Yet, sometimes this proves essential.

Leadership Styles

While there are many more descriptions of what leadership entails, I want to keep things simple and define two essential styles of leadership: push or pull. One way is to push people to get the results required, and the other is to learn to inspire people, so they want to do their best, and, beyond that, use initiative and take responsibility to get things done.

The Skill Sets of Leaders

Acquiring a leadership role can have its own challenges. Studies show that as many as 8-9 newly promoted executives and leaders get fired or demoted within three years. As many as 8 entrepreneurs out of 10 fail within the first 18 months, and an average of 65% of SMEs—small-medium enterprises—close their doors within 5 years. So what could possibly be the problem? Internal wiring, of course.

It would be useful to consider that, maintaining any position, aside from the relevant skills required, can call for a different kind of mindset and even attitude.[28] As mentioned before, the Pareto principle, although not an exact science, helps us to realise that while skills are essential, they can never make up for personal resilience, which account for the 80% internal wiring we have been studying throughout this whole book. Whether we are talking about a department in an organisation, or a solo-preneur, the results produced are always an extension of the person behind the project.

Let's look at the elements that may hinder or contribute to developing excellence in leadership roles and entrepreneurial success.

---

[28] See *What Got You Here Won't Get You There*, a book by Marshall Goldsmith.

BUILDING RESILIENCE IN LEADERSHIP

Negative Habits	Positive Habits
Blaming	Taking responsibility
Cutting across / finishing other people's phrases	Waiting to speak in turn / allow each to express fully
One-upmanship	Acknowledging others
Correcting people in public	Observing respect and confidentiality
Thinking we have all the answers	Welcoming others' views and input
Making excuses	Stating facts, describing as they are and not embellished
Clinging to past achievement	Clarity, awareness and foresight in the moment
Being ungrateful	Acknowledgement and praise
Verbal superiority 'but', 'this won't work because . . .'	Listening to other's point of view—Keeping an opened mind
Playing favourites	Appreciating each person for who they are
Lacking accountability	Welcoming / accepting feedback

ESSENTIAL LEADERSHIP SKILL n.1: Communication

On the path of developing resilience in leadership, or entrepreneurship, one of the most important skills to develop is communication. Many people understandably lack this simple skill, as this is another powerful tool that was not taught in our educational system. Yet, communication alone can 'miraculously' solve most situations in the shortest amount of time possible. It carries the all-important element of information required for negotiation, bettering any situation, or developing a service or product. In short, to insure that success is a more certain outcome.

All communication is precious, powerful and essential. If you are a leader, engaging in dialogue with your employees, or the HR department, means that you are using some of your finer leadership skills and assets. If you are an entrepreneur, engaging in dialogue with your clients can literally make or break your business. It can be shocking to realise that no one is interested in a product or service that we hoped would be a total winner, just because we are personally invested in it. I can't think of any challenge in any situation that will not benefit from real communication.

Almost all leadership concerns discussed here can be useful when applied to parenting.[29] You will find that these can contribute to keeping communication opened

---

[29] See the list of resilience skills at the end of this chapter

on both sides, which will become pertinent by the time your children reach their teenage years. You may have gone through these years already.

As a parent, someone they look up to, it is up to you to lead by example and set the communication standards that will inspire them to want to talk to you. Remember, while the communication is opened, you still have a 'card' to play. When communication ceases, it can create serious division. We already saw that 'a house divided cannot stand', and parenting is no exclusion to this.

Our kids are way smarter and faster than we are, as they carry the new 'mental wiring' that is typical of any new generation. Since electronic communication has blown past all limits and will continue to do so, it is particularly important to cultivate human communication. Kids are amazingly wise and can help you to transform some of your own programming so you can free yourself. But you have to go first, like a true leader. You may look again at the table above with 'parenting eyes' and see if there are some elements you might like to use, delete or reinforce.

We will focus on two major aspects of communication here: the first is listening; and the second, talking. There are, of course, many other aspects of communication, for example body language, or what is 'unsaid' but gets picked up energetically anyway, that we could explore. You will find that, as you take care of yourself in terms of your own practise, many other things will correct themselves.

So whether you work as a leader, or want to use these skills for your own personal life, you will find the following invaluable.

We begin with listening skills, as we have two ears and only one mouth. There may be a message in the design!

Listening Skills

Due to a variety of factors, most of us don't listen to one another when we talk to each other. We may be too busy or too distracted to give anyone our full attention. Yet, listening closely, in presence, is a valuable skill to learn. Listening skills can prevent or resolve conflicts in our professional life, and help us to build intimacy in our close relationships.

As you browse through the different styles of listening below, you might identify one or more of these as your tendencies.

While listening to someone, do you usually:

- Wait until you can speak and bring up a story about someone else or something about you that sounds like what you are hearing?

- Hold on so tight to what you want to say or what you are going to answer back that you don't really hear what is being said?

- Not listen, tune out?

- Validate what you already know, and not really

hear what is being imparted?

- Have mental chatter, such as comparing, judging, evaluating, etc.?
- Expect to know what you are going to hear and therefore not receive what is being offered?
- Pretend to listen, but know full well that you are not willing to budge or take what is being said on-board?

None of the above are useful to deepening the communication or inviting any collaboration from a colleague, or for that matter, a beloved. In fact, and particularly, communication is required for conflict prevention or attempting conflict resolution, the listed actions above will nearly always make things worse.

Here is what you can do instead:

- Tune in to your B.B.C. to regain full internal and external awareness, which will afford you to feel as present as you can be.
- If strong emotions, judgements and beliefs arise in you as a result of what you are hearing, you obviously are 'invested' in what is being said. Take the opportunity to free yourself from the programmes you are feeling coming up in you by using your DELETE button, or mentally saying or thinking, 'I release you from . . .'
- As you are remaining aware and present, when

the time comes, you may be inspired to speak in a more dispassionate way that can be more beneficial to both of you, devoid of strong emotions or temper, criticism or judgement.

- Even if what you say ends up being the same as what you were going to say, the energetic charge behind your words will be very different. This insures that the best of you is being expressed, stating facts without drama.

- You may find yourself asking additional questions, to be able to get to the root of what you hear, which is inviting collaboration to deeper conversation.

This can insure that the person in front of you feels heard and validated, sometimes without you even needing to say anything. Non-action is sometimes the best course of action. Although energy is not clearly visible between people, we can certainly all feel it. We can all feel when someone is present to our conversation, although, we may not be able to articulate it. Presence invites wisdom, and you may be surprised to know exactly what to say, once you are fully present.

Q&A

Q: In a situation with potential conflict, for example, during a board meeting, what is the point of using the practices learnt here if I am going to end up saying the same as what I was going to say anyway?

A: The answer lies in the question. If you already know what you are going to say, you are probably not being as present as you could be during the meeting, therefore, not as receptive as you could be to the input being offered. You are not allowing the necessary 'movement' in the conversation that could spell the difference between negotiation and conflict. Deciding what you are going to answer *no matter what* actually means that your mind is already made up, and the 'deal' is 'sealed'.

When I mentioned earlier that you might end up answering the same thing as you originally thought, it included keeping an open mind throughout the meeting. If you can let go of your original idea for a little while, you will find it easier to be more receptive to others' input. The fact that you may end up saying the same as you suspected is then circumstantial rather than strategic.

For example, if you decide to use your tools to remain truly present, and to delete your programming when you feel a strong reaction come up in you, you may find it easier to hear different points of view. You may even find that some of them can be useful to resolving the situation at hand.

In case you end up saying the same thing you originally thought, the words spoken will be said in the best possible way, meaning, with a different kind of energy behind it. It is possible to express a completely different meaning with the same words in the same order, depending on our intention, state of presence, feelings, energy, tone of voice, facial expressions, etc.

Having reconnected to your innermost resources means that your message will have a considerably different impact on all those around you. Even if a tough decision has to be made, people are always willing to be more understanding when they feel heard, taken into consideration, valued, and appreciated. Most people are very extremely sensitive to small nuances, more than you can imagine. Your leadership skills literally depend on your own internal wiring, and the expression of the same. These skills can make a difference in your ability to inspire, foster or develop a strong, powerful and collaborative work culture.

Q: If I practise my full NeuroBiology Reprogramming™, including all 3 steps while I listen to someone, does it not mean that I am self-absorbed and not paying attention?

A: I love that question. It often comes up. When you practice N.B.R., you will find that it takes far less involvement to think DELETE or 'I release you from . . .' to a programme, than the usual and constant internal commentary that goes on while you listen. When you use N.B.R., you are merely harnessing your mind rather than letting it run riot. The truth is that the mind never stops, or at least not until it is trained to be in a state of stillness, or walking meditation, as is the effect of using your B.B.M.E. practice.

There is nothing about self-indulgence in becoming as present as you can be, and taking care of clearing what comes up in your mind, so you can be more receptive to your interlocutor. Quite the contrary. The more present and receptive you are, the more they can benefit. People can often hear their own solution when they can express what they need to say and be fully received or heard. This is a rare and precious opportunity for many, as most people are too preoccupied to truly listen to anyone.

Sadly, being heard often requires the services of a therapist of some sort, or a coach. Some people do really know how to listen, of course, but this is often a learned skill. From now on, unless, of course, you can already listen in presence, this can be you.

I cannot think of any situation where you and your interlocutor will not benefit, whether you are a CEO, a doctor, a therapist, a parent, a partner, or a friend. Listening attentively, being fully present, works in any and all situations.

A win-win practice.

Talking Skills

As you cultivate internal awareness, you will begin to notice your own verbal habits, and how you interact during conversations. As with all previous tools and steps in this section, this will allow you to develop leadership skills that you will find invaluable when applied to your professional life. You will find these equally useful for your personal relationships, including your parenting.

The aim of becoming aware about your own style of dialogue is simply to gain clarity and foresight, so you can make important shifts if necessary. It is not in the least about beating yourself up or getting lost in guilt, as these would be self-indulgent rather than useful, going back to past situations, which you can do nothing about.

Just like all other habits we replay unconsciously, our habitual conversation mode and manner of speaking was learnt when we were young, and along the way, very much subconsciously. Like all other programmes, this can be cleared and replaced with a more favourable tone of expression. Applied to leadership, this will undoubtedly contribute to developing integrity, grace and dignity. As we develop the ability to take responsibility in all ways possible, it allows others to do the same. This can completely transform a culture at work, or the environment back in our family and with our children.

In the name of simplicity and usability, I have classified conversation in two distinct styles: collaborative conversation and accusative conversation.

Collaborative Communication Versus Accusative Communication

Imagine that someone is saying to you:

> 'You didn't understand what I was saying.'

How does that make you feel? This comment means that you are lacking the capacity to understand what was being said to you. So you might be feeling 'dim-witted', perhaps, as this puts the blame on you . . . not so nice at all. At least, not coming from a leader.

Instead, a leader would take responsibility and say:

> 'I didn't express myself very well, please allow me to explain.'

How does that make you feel? Much better, yes? This is because, in this case, the leader is not making you wrong in any way. The conversation can be far more collaborative, and unfold in a much more favourable way, producing much better end results. Remember, people are far more sensitive than you can imagine.

Now this time, imagine that the leader is you, and that you are saying to your interlocutor:

'What are you trying to say?'

How do you think your interlocutor feels? Very likely like a 'mumbling fool' as you are putting the misunderstanding on their side, rather than yours. Whether this is what you meant or not, this is how it will be perceived.

Instead, you could say:

'I am not sure I understand you correctly; could you repeat please?'

Taking responsibility for misunderstanding what is being said will allow your interlocutor to express what they need to say. If you are the leader, you can imagine that they might be feeling nervous as it is, and that it may have taken them a lot of courage to even come up and talk to you in the first place. If they are already partly in a fight-or-flight mode—perhaps due to what is going on for them and why they are talking to you—this could make them even more anxious, which means that they are literally drowning in stress hormones. The result of such stress means that they may effectively feel completely unable to convey anything coherently. So this would be a great opportunity to use every leadership skill you have, as many people do not do well under extreme stress.

4 WAYS TO PREPARE FOR CLEAR COMMUNICATION

1. Personal resourcefulness—Resilience

Whether the phone is ringing or someone is knocking at the door, take a few seconds to tune in to your own B.B.C., to reconnect with your core self. The phone can always ring one more time, and there can always be one more knock at the door. We all tend to be on high alert constantly, jumping to read texts or answer calls, which means that we let ourselves be constantly manipulated by technology and other people. This reduces our attention span and our ability to be present to ourselves, and each other.

2. Approachability

Ask yourself if you are approachable? For this, you can go back to the self-inquiry exercises we did in the mental resilience and emotional resilience chapters. Realising where you live mentally, and therefore emotionally, will give you some insight as to the quality of your life. Again, don't beat yourself up if you find that this needs to improve. Just use your clearing tools and move on. We all have programming. When we know better, we do better. Be willing to set yourself free!

3. Accuracy

Say things as they are, and resist the urge to dramatise or embellish them. There is a very big difference between describing facts and telling a tale, where you may be the victim or the hero. This is particularly useful if you are dealing with a potentially confrontational situation. As Tony Robbins says, *"It doesn't matter how thin you slice it, there are always two sides to any story!"* This is a powerful realisation that can allow for fairness and resolution.

4. Clarity

Clarity is key. There are two aspects to this. The first is to make sure we actually communicate. Too often, we assume that someone knows or understands something, when, in fact, they have no idea, largely due to the fact we may not have expressed ourselves clearly or accurately enough. Let's assume that no one is psychic! Also it is worth taking into consideration that everyone has busy schedules, and 'assuming' that there will be time often means there is none left when finally required, at the last minute. Asking for confirmation of a message received is a proactive, simple and very useful habit.

Do Try This at Home!

Not so strangely, taking this simple suggestion back home and expressing your gratitude, love and appreciation for family members or your spouse can do much to improve everyone's life quality. I often hear people say, 'He or she knows I love them'. While that might be true, I can't think of anyone who does not enjoy feeling significant or appreciated. Daily. Again, assume that no one has psychic power, even if they do!

Trading Marshmallow-Talk for Self-Directedness

The way we express ourselves says much about us. There is a style of communication that I call 'marshmallow communication'. It is using words that reflect uncertainty, and the inability to have self-direction.

Although particularly relevant to develop leadership-style communication, this will benefit many other situations as it puts across a sense of confidence, self-directedness and mutual respect. Let's say that you have been invited for dinner.

Here is what NOT to say:

- 'I'll try and be there.' It is best to keep the word 'trying' for when we need to fit a pair of shoes or pants we are considering buying!

- 'I hope to be there.' It is best to save this type of answer for a time when we have a serious illness and might die in the meantime. Hopefully never!

- 'Maybe . . .' This is as vague as the sea. It makes the person who invited you feel unimportant.

- 'I should' or 'I shouldn't'. Best to take a moment to make a decision, and then stick to it. Should and shouldn't mean that something outside of us has the power to overturn our decision or has the power, instead of us, to direct our life.

Instead of all the above, we can choose a more direct style of communication, which includes clarity and precision. The following style of conversation reflects self-directedness and clarity. It is typical of someone who has leadership or a winner's qualities.

- 'I'll be there' or 'I won't be able to make it because . . .' or 'I'll do what it takes to get it done' or 'Is this a deadline or is there some leeway for the completion date?' instead of 'I'll try'.

- 'Let me get back to you when I know for certain' instead of 'I hope to be there.'

- 'Yes' or 'No' instead of 'Maybe', or 'Let me check my diary and get back to you.'

- 'I have decided to' instead of 'I should' or 'I shouldn't'.

ESSENTIAL LEADERSHIP SKILL n.2: Personal Values and Standards

Values and standards are effectively the programmes we carry that we have learnt along the way, and, like most of them, during our childhood. Many of these values are really good, and even complementary when applied to particular areas in our lives. However, a value that works wonders when applied to our accounts can spell disaster in our relationships. Yet, this often happens simply because it is an easy mistake to make. It is more likely that we apply the same values we hold dear across the board. Here are some examples.

Example 1

'Control' is a fantastic value when applied to one's own mind, personal accounts and finances, for example. It can be devastating, however, if applied to a relationship with our spouse or partner.

Example 2

'Security' can be a great value when applied to being responsible and taking care of our children. However, the same value can become a stumbling block if that same person wants to become an entrepreneur. Not having the insurance and the security that a paycheck provides at the end of the month can be too much uncertainty for some people. The amount of personal trust, confidence, courage, and resilience necessary to drive an enterprise forward is not for everyone. Many prefer the guaranteed income that being employed provides. There is nothing wrong with that, quite the contrary, but self-clarity is king. If that person decides that they want to pursue entrepreneurship in spite of a serious need of security, it is 100% possible, especially if using NeuroBiology Reprogramming™ to gain maximum resilience. Forewarned is forearmed.

Now apply this same value, 'security', to a relationship. This could mean that the need for—financial—security holds a relationship together that no longer serves the growth of the union, or the individual growth of each partner.

Example 3

'Perfectionism' can be great for anyone who wants to do a job to the highest standard possible. However, expecting perfection in ourselves, with our own image, or from someone else is setting ourselves up for a fall.

Perfection is the is-ness of life. It reflects the moment, which, even if deemed unsatisfactory, still provides the perfect ground for us to see that something needs to change.

EXERCISE
Your Personal Values

The following exercise is done in two parts. It is designed to give you some insight as to what your values are, and where some may need to be cleared, or reallocated, depending on whether they are a help or a hindrance.

Part 1: Have a look at the list of values below,[30] and take a moment to circle 3-12 of your most important ones.

---

[30] Reproduced with permission from www.mindtools.com.

- Accountability
- Accuracy
- Achievement
- Adventure
- Altruism
- Ambition
- Assertiveness
- Balance
- Being the best
- Belonging
- Boldness
- Calmness
- Carefulness
- Challenge
- Cheerfulness
- Clear-mindedness
- Commitment
- Community
- Compassion
- Competitiveness
- Consistency
- Contentment
- Continuous Improvement
- Contribution
- Control
- Cooperation
- Correctness
- Courtesy
- Excellence
- Excitement
- Expertise
- Exploration
- Expressiveness
- Fairness
- Faith
- Family-orientedness
- Fidelity
- Fitness
- Fluency
- Focus
- Freedom
- Fun
- Generosity
- Goodness
- Grace
- Growth
- Happiness
- Hard Work
- Health
- Helping Society
- Holiness
- Honesty
- Honor
- Humility
- Independence
- Ingenuity
- Inner Harmony
- Perfection
- Piety
- Positivity
- Practicality
- Preparedness
- Professionalism
- Prudence
- Quality-orientation
- Reliability
- Resourcefulness
- Restraint
- Results-oriented
- Rigor
- Security
- Self-actualization
- Self-control
- Selflessness
- Self-reliance
- Sensitivity
- Serenity
- Service
- Shrewdness
- Simplicity
- Soundness
- Speed
- Spontaneity
- Stability
- Strategic

Creativity	Inquisitiveness	Strength
Curiosity	Insightfulness	Structure
Decisiveness	Intelligence	Success
Democraticness	Intellectual	Support
Dependability	Status	Teamwork
Determination	Intuition	Temperance
Devoutness	Joy	Thankfulness
Diligence	Justice	Thoroughness
Discipline	Leadership	Thoughtfulness
Discretion	Legacy	Timeliness
Diversity	Love	Tolerance
Dynamism	Loyalty	Traditionalism
Economy	Making a	Trustworthiness
Effectiveness	difference	Truth-seeking
Efficiency	Mastery	Understanding
Elegance	Merit	Uniqueness
Empathy	Obedience	Unity
Enjoyment	Openness	Usefulness
Enthusiasm	Order	Vision
Equality	Originality	Vitality
	Patriotism	

Part Two: Next, and depending on what area of your Wheel of Life you wanted to improve or take to the next level, ask yourself if these same values benefit or limit you in some way. Use the following questions and the 8-step process below.

The areas explored on the Wheel of Life: 'How Smooth Is Your Ride' exercise were:

- Physical health, energy, mojo
- Finances, money management
- Job, career, mission
- Time management
- Relationships & communication with others
- Self-worth, self-confidence, self-appreciation
- Celebration, contribution
- Self-discipline / spiritual practice

9-Step Process Exercise

1. Write the area(s) you chose here. If there are several you would like to examine, do one at a time:

   -

   -

   -

2. Looking at the values you circled, do you think that they contribute or take away from your intended plans in your chosen area?

   Contribute – Take Away

3. If contribute, which one, and how do they help you?

    -

    -

    -

4. If take away, which one, and why do they limit you?

    -

    -

    -

5. Proceed with clearing the values that are holding you up in your chosen area of improvement using your DELETE key or 'I release you from . . .':

    -

    -

    -

6. What values do you need to install or transfer to another area to make sure that you can create the results you want to experience?

    -

    -

    -

7. **Write down 1-3 actual action steps you need to make to move closer to what you want to experience, as you outlined in 6.**

   -

   -

   -

8. **Write down 1-3 actual action steps you are going to take to implement your new values.**

   -

   -

   -

9. **Pick a starting date for the above.** (Hint: Why do tomorrow what you can do today? There is no time like the present!)

   -

   -

   -

You are amazing!

RESILIENCE IN PARENTING

These are popular during classes. Here is a sample of resilience tools for parents.

1. Teach your kids that the stronger anyone is, the kinder and gentler they are because they don't have anything to prove.
2. Don't use comparison amongst siblings or anyone else.
3. Beyond baby and toddler years, see yourself as a guardian more than a parent, it will help them become more independent, and you less controlling.
4. Talk to them with the same respect you expect from them.
5. Never end the day without making up, no matter how serious an issue may be. Share words of love and forgiveness, always.
6. Apologise when an apology is due.
7. Focus on the positive result, and discuss the negative. Get clarity as to what help they might need to do better, from you or someone else.
8. Don't be afraid of showing some vulnerability—this is how they learn that it is ok for them to feel that way too, they won't need to 'use crutches' later on in life.

9. Beyond the age of 10 or 11, and perhaps before, ask them if they would like to organise their own routine, in particular their homework planning. Ask them if they are willing to take full responsibility for it and pay the consequence in school if need be. Or would they rather have you monitoring and organising for them?

10. Love yourself—their self-esteem depends on yours.

11. Install and reward initiative; make a huge deal of it when it happens.

12. Let them find their own solutions; they are far more creative than any adult.

13. Teach them the law of cause and effect instead of punishing them. This is your job for a limited time; after that, it is between the world and them.

14. Tell them they are loveable and don't need to be or do anything other than themselves to be worthy of love.

15. Encourage them to follow their passion, but best if you do it too!

16. Tell them they are enough just being who they are, they are perfect, and they have many gifts and talents they may not be aware of yet.

17. At any age, don't keep repeating worry-filled statements to them: 'Get down the stairs, you'll

fall. Get down the stairs, you'll fall; get down the stairs, you'll fall!' Then they fall. Then you say, 'Told you!' This is how you build fear, deplete resilience, teach them to not trust themselves, and, instead, count on someone outside themselves to know what steps to take. Use your clearing tools instead.

18. When you need to correct something, make sure you separate the behaviour from the person, and make sure they understand that; explain it to them.

19. Don't lie to your kids; this is what fragments the mind early on. They perceive below conscious level, so it is better if your words and explanations are congruent with the reality you are living / the reality in the household. Kids don't listen to words as much as they duplicate our habits and behaviour.

20. Focus on what's right instead of what's wrong. When they run back because they forgot their lunch box, say, 'What did you just remember?' not 'What did you forget?'

21. Teach them HOW to think and not WHAT to think. Keep your opinions to yourself; there is probably too much programming in there!

22. Do teach them about the 3 different types of fear, so they can distinguish and naturally let their own level of resilience increase.

23. Get over any guilt, self-hatred, resentment, criticism, etc. as soon as possible, and clear out your own programmes if you see or hear some of them in your kids. Don't teach them to clear their programming; the programming is in you, that is why you can see it in them. This is how you will set yourself and your kids free.

24. Remind them (if necessary) that they were completely able to take their first few steps, when they decided to do so. They didn't give up at any point. If they fell, they simply tried another way: on all-fours, on their bum, grabbing onto a chair, anything at all, but they got it done. When they 'fail' at something, it just outlines that they found one more way that didn't work out, and 'it'—whatever they are wanting to achieve—is still very much on the menu. All they need to do is to find another way. It will always work out.

25. Beyond this, want to teach your kids resilience? BE IT. Want to teach your kids mindfulness? BE IT. Want to teach your kids to clear their programming? DON'T! What you see out there is in you. Be everything that you can be; this is how you teach, this is how they learn, by subconscious duplication. Remember the security announcement on the plane: "Put your own oxygen mask on first!"

LET'S TALK STORY . . . ONE LAST TIME!

From Our Friend, Nasruddin

While on a trip to another village, Nasruddin lost his favourite copy of the mystical book.

Several weeks later, a goat walked up to Nasruddin, carrying the book in its mouth.

Nasruddin couldn't believe his eyes. He took the precious book out of the goat's mouth, raised his eyes heavenward and exclaimed, 'It's a miracle!'

'Not really,' said the goat, 'your name is written inside the cover.'

CHAPTER 9—CHAPTER RECAP

THE HEART OF LEADERSHIP

Building Resilience In Leadership

Essential Leadership Skill n.1:
Communication

Essential Leadership Skill n.2:
Values and Standards

Resilience In Parenting

CHAPTER 10

REVERSE ENGINEERING

"One can have no smaller or greater mastery than mastery of oneself."

— Leonardo da Vinci

Reverse Engineering for the Mind: The Ultimate Resilience and Self-Mastery Tool

Now that you know exactly how your mind functions, and how to clear it, you are ready for the Master Plan!

Consider this for a second: there are several recurring questions in you, a part of your daily self-talk. These are usually not very complimentary, which means that you are cementing already existing programmes. This can effectively sabotage your resilience and, with it, your ability to create the success you really want to experience.

You know by now that emotions always follow thoughts, and that the two combined create feelings, which become beliefs. Beliefs are just like seeking missiles, they will find and lock onto what they recognise, as directed by the mind. Remember the exercise we did earlier on, where I had you look around the room for yellow objects. It is vital that you identify what your recurring questions are, because they are instructing your mind to seek and find the evidence of what you are telling yourself.

Here are some examples:
- Why am I so bad at . . .?
- Why am I so broke?
- Why am I such a lousy lover, friend, etc.?
- Why do I always fail at . . .?
- Why can't I achieve . . .?
- Why does . . . keep eluding me?

You get the idea. Take a moment to identify your recurring questions, and in the meantime, here is a story.

The Power of the Mind—Story

In 1943, upon taking a picture of his 3-year-old daughter, Dr. Edwin Land was asked by the inquisitive, curious and impatient young child, 'Dad, why can't I see the picture now, I want to see it now!' Although the story goes that he took the time to explain the process through which the picture could be produced, he did not dismiss her inquiry. It was his desire to produce a seemingly impossible result, to please his daughter, that gave him the drive to keep asking himself the same question. *How could the picture be instantly visible?*

The answer had no other choice but to come to him, and he invented the Polaroid camera.

Quick Path to Success

There are two enormous gifts in this story. The first is that all the resilience in the world will become available to you when you seek to serve a cause beyond your own interest. This is the essence of the heart of leadership.

The second gift contained in this story is the art of asking ourselves empowering questions. If we reverse engineer the power and ability of the mind with the right question, there is nothing that we cannot accomplish. This is exciting! Allow me to explain.

EXERCISE
The Art of Asking Self-Empowering Questions

Think about the original area you wanted to improve, or take to the next level, and see what your recurring question might be, regarding it, if you had one. If this is not obvious at first glance, please allow some time and use your B.B.C. or your B.B.M.E. to relax. You may need to do a little digging, or you may know straight away what you repeatedly tell yourself. Once you have it, go ahead and reverse engineer that question.

Let me give you an example. If the former question was 'Why am I always so broke?', the new question could be 'How am I making so much money on a constant basis, and keeping some so easily?'

If you asked, 'Why am I always attracting women or men that are unavailable?', you could swap it for 'How am easily meeting people that are open to long-term partnership?'

Don't forget that once the internal work is done, you will need to take a step in the direction of what you have declared. But please forget about consciously looking for the answer, as this will be answered in the form of inspiration. This is actually really important. Think of it this way, you are naming the 'what' and the 'why'. Stay out of your own way to be able to receive the 'how'. In short, once you have your question, 'let go' of wanting to control the situation. You just gave the 'coordinates' to your mind-missile, now sit back and steer yourself in the direction that you feel called to pursue, moment by moment. One day at a time. You can listen in to any parts of your internal guidance, including intuition, inspiration or gut feeling.

You can repeat your question anytime the old one comes to mind, and even bring it up 10-30 times per day, or whenever you think of it. This is how you can quickly actualise business ideas, goals and other things you want to achieve or experience.

Here are some useful additional questions that I often use when in need of directional inspiration:

- What am I not hearing / seeing / feeling regarding this . . . (particular project, situation, person, opportunity, etc.)?

- What is the best next step I need to take, if any?

- What do I need to release from my mindset so I can actualise this heart's desire?

- What qualities or mindset do I need to take on-board or learn to achieve . . . ?

- What do I need to stop doing or give up to be able to . . . ?

MASTER TOOL

This is the ultimate mind-shift, and the fastest way to actualising the ideas that you hold in thought-form. It can potentially turn your reality around in an instant, and shatter any doubt or feelings that 'things may not work out'. Are you ready?

Please look at the following drawing. It is yet another way the mind can be depicted. The tiny, dark arrow at the bottom depicts the conscious mind.

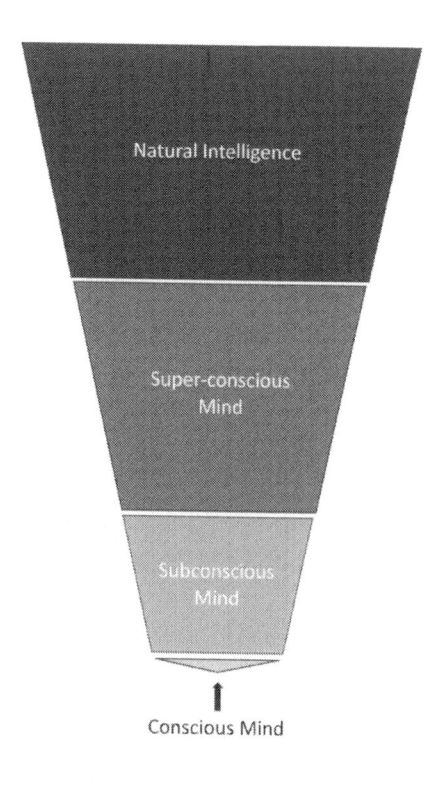

You know how we have been talking about the fact that, within the mind, the conscious mind is the last part of us to be aware of what is really taking place in our whole being? This is important.

Natural Intelligence is always connected to the super-conscious mind, which is itself connected to the subconscious mind. All of this takes care of keeping our innermost intricate biological systems finetuned and closely functioning so we can breathe, digest, our heart can beat, etc. Whether we are conscious of it or not at all, all of this keeps on functioning. As mentioned previously, the conscious mind is the last one to know anything, remember, this is my favourite cosmic joke!

Here it is . . . so pay close attention!

Let's say that you just got a brilliant business idea. If it is really brilliant, this idea is inspired, meaning that it is coming from the Natural Intelligence part of you. This is amazing, as it is how every bestseller, work of art, innovation, invention, and extremely successful idea was created.

Now I need to repeat this: remember the conscious mind is the last part of us to become aware of what the rest of our being already knows, okay? This means that you wouldn't be able to even think this idea UNLESS it was already part of your experience. Are you with me?

So the fact that your conscious mind is finally aware of it MEANS THAT IT IS ALREADY DONE. We are here for the journey, to experience ourselves as the Creators that we are. The fun of it is in actualising the vision or the idea you have just received. This makes a very big difference. One way is to think that the conscious mind alone worked really hard to come up with the idea—which usually involves far too much ego—and that we then have to fret to make it happen. Or the other way, much closer to the truth, is that the idea was given to us, and we had better stay out of the way, clearing our own limitations as they arise, to be able to hear direction, and take steps in the direction of success. If it is already done, why fret?

You are here to experience yourself and have fun in the process, tapping into your potential, Connecting the DOTS™ to make the most of your Creator's ability. This leaves us with only one question: Can you let it in?

If you said 'YES', then do these three things:

1. This idea is already on the way since you just got the information from your mind. Simply DELETE any limiting beliefs as they arise, and stay present using your B.B.C. to recognise the best ways to actualise your idea.

2. MOVE in the direction of making it happen when you feel called. Any direction is better than sitting down doing nothing. Remember each attempt that doesn't work brings you closer to the one that will. Bear in mind that any 'overnight success' is the result of a lifetime of practise.

3. ENJOY the journey, because when this is done, you will be onto the next thing. This is because your human potential is vast, and the possibilities and probabilities of existence are many. Your nature and your inevitable purpose is to create products, services, art, ideas, etc., and the side effect of this is your receiving sustenance in the form of finances, etc.

PARTING NOTE

If you are reading these lines right now, it means that you are an absolute winner! Studies show that most people read the first 10-30% of any book and then drop it. You didn't, so I want to tell you that you have what it takes to take your life to the next level, without a shadow of a doubt.

A heartfelt 'thank you' for choosing to pick up this book, and reading it to the end. I sincerely hope that it is of benefit to you, and that it will help you get all the resilience you need, so you can get everything you want.

You will have changed effortlessly while reading because new neural pathways have literally been created as you resonated with some of what you read. This is pretty exciting! This is also why there is an amount of repetition throughout the book.

If you choose to read over it another time, which I highly recommend, your subconscious will receive another download of the information included and all of it will become more probable. You will also read things that you may not have noticed the first time.

If you choose to use the 3 steps offered, you will develop bulletproof resilience. That is a personal guarantee. It means that you have just committed to making your life an extraordinary journey and a masterpiece.

I invite you to sign up at my main website, and to check out what is available right now. NeuroBiology

Reprogramming™ is available online once a year, and available as part of a 'Private Intensive' programme I offer, which includes coaching and clearing sessions. There are some guided meditations and a few other exercises that could not be included in a book.

NeuroBiology Reprogramming™ is also available as a practitioner and teacher training.

I very much look forward to hearing from you. I would greatly appreciate a review on Amazon.

Please join me at my official Facebook page, look for Dr. Dugast, to share your experiences, as I would love to hear from you and you can receive daily inspirational quotes and messages.

Thank you again from the bottom of my heart for taking the time to invest in yourself, and for understanding the importance and potential that this personal science offers.

You are amazing! Don't you ever forget it.

Yours in success,

Mahayana

ABOUT THE AUTHOR

Dr. Dugast was born in Chamonix-Mont-Blanc, France.

She is an international speaker, author, healer, and executive coach.

She has practised and taught self-realisation methods, natural medicine, clearings/healings, and personal development for the past 30 years. She is a doctor of Metaphysical Sciences, and the founder of NeuroBiology Reprogramming™, a practitioner and teacher training.

Her signature seminar is Connecting the DOTS™.

OTHER TITLES FROM DR. DUGAST

Available in all formats direct from Amazon

Mahayana's Rejuvenating Manual

Rejuvenating Trilogy

MIND REVOLUTION: Connecting the DOTS

ONLINE RESOURCES

Individual Consultations—Coaching—Clearings/Healings

Practitioner & Teacher Training & License NeuroBiology Reprogramming™

Visit www.drdugast.com

CORPORATE

Corporate engagements

Executive coaching

In-person Retreats & Private Intensive Programmes

Visit www.corporatemindfulness.ie / www.corporatemindfulness.co.uk

Printed in Great Britain
by Amazon